monsoonbooks

PRAYING TO THE GODDESS OF MERCY

Hailing from Singapore, Mahita Vas struggled for years with what she now knows were manic highs and depressive lows. She credits her husband, children, friends and her daily dosage of lithium for providing an essential element of balance.

T0098296

PRAYING TO THE GODDESS OF MERCY

A MEMOIR OF MOOD SWINGS

MAHITA VAS

monsoon

monsoonbooks

Published in 2012
by Monsoon Books Pte Ltd, 71 Ayer Rajah Crescent #01-01
Mediapolis Phase Ø, Singapore 139951
www.monsoonbooks.com.sg

ISBN (paperback): 978-981-4358-91-0
ISBN (ebook): 978-981-4358-92-7

Copyright©Mahita Vas, 2012
The moral right of the author has been asserted.

All rights reserved. No part of this publication may be reproduced, stored in a retrieval system, or transmitted, in any form or by any means without the prior written permission of the publisher, nor be otherwise circulated in any form of binding or cover other than that in which it is published and without a similar condition being imposed on the subsequent purchaser.

Cover design by Alessandra David.
Title art by Daniel Hochard, Imagex Fonts

National Library Board, Singapore Cataloguing-in-Publication Data
Vas, Mahita.
Praying to the Goddess of Mercy : a memoir of mood swings / Mahita Vas. – Singapore : Monsoon Books, 2012.
p. cm.
ISBN : 978-981-4358-91-0 (pbk.)
1. Vas, Mahita – Mental health. 2. Manic-depressive persons – Singapore – Biography. I. Title.
RC516
616.8950092 -- dc23   OCN797986649

Produced with the support of

Media Development Authority
Singapore

Printed in Singapore
15 14 13 12   1 2 3 4 5

For
Madam Cheong Lau Kin,
Beloved Amah, Rest In Peace
and
Susan Henkel Smith

AUTHOR'S NOTE

This is a true story about mental illness. To maintain the focus on the illness itself, most of the events and situations described are relevant to manic or depressive episodes which had a direct impact on my actions and emotions.

There have been countless instances of unusual behaviour due to my manic or depressive phases since my teenage years. I cannot possibly list them all. Similarly, I have also experienced many stretches of normalcy; good and bad occurrences during those times have been selectively included, tied to a bigger story in any given chapter. Without doubt, my life has been affected by various events, but the exclusion of some of those events does not compromise or change my story as it relates to mental illness; it is this illness which is at the heart and soul of this book.

Most of the dialogue was reconstructed around what I could remember of a specific line or a semblance of what was said. The intent in all conversations remains true.

I relied heavily on my memory to write this book and understand that some people involved may have a different recollection of these same events and situations.

The names of my immediate family and some others have been changed.

CHAPTER 1

'When we lose the right to be different,
we lose the privilege to be free.'
Charles Evans Hughes

My first memory of smell is Amah's crisp white cotton tunic, which she hand-washed and starched daily. My first memory of touch, her silky soft black loose pants clenched in my fingers and then being let go, as I watched the fabric bloom back into shape.

I was born in the Year of the Tiger barely three years before Singapore's independence in 1965. My Hindu parents from India – a deeply religious mother from pre-partition Karachi and a volatile father from Kerala – left the day-to-day care of my older sister and me to Amah, our Cantonese nanny.

Like all domestic servants from China at the time, she was called Amah, a respectful name for the Chinese live-in help who was also the cook and nanny. Amah was fifty years old when she held me in her arms. I was three days old and had just arrived from hospital. We could not have foreseen the strong bond we would share and the immense cultural influence she would have on me long into adulthood.

In the bedroom we shared, Amah had a statue of Guan Yin, the Goddess of Mercy, whom I always thought in my young mind was the prettiest goddess. She was prettier than the Hindu goddesses on my mother's altar: Lakshmi, the Goddess of Wealth, resplendent in her embroidered robes in rich gold and red, and Saraswati, the Goddess of Knowledge, beautiful with her milky-white skin, draped in a silk and gold saree, standing on a swan. That was before I saw a picture of the Virgin Mary with blonde hair, blue eyes and looking at her baby Jesus; I thought she was the prettiest goddess in the world. When it was pointed out to me that the Virgin Mary was not a goddess, Guan Yin resumed her position in my mind as the prettiest goddess in the whole world. For years I wondered why Mary was not a goddess and just accepted the explanation I was given at my Catholic school that she was Jesus' mummy.

With my Indian Hindu parents and Chinese nanny as my main caregivers, and educated in a Catholic school with girls who formed Singapore's racial mix of Chinese, Malay, Indian and Eurasian, I grew up in a rich multi-cultural, multi-religious environment. Due to Amah's stronger and more positive influence on me, I grew up feeling more Chinese than Indian and spent afternoons watching Cantonese soap operas on television. They were mainly produced in Hong Kong and followed a simple formula which was invariably rehashed with slight variations.

Man or woman from lower income background meets woman or man from privileged family and falls in love. Against all odds and amidst some kind of tragedy in between, they are united in the end.

Every weekday afternoon just before three o'clock, Amah would plant her rattan chair, slightly worn at the seat, in front of the television and sit still for an hour. Occasionally, she would fall asleep, head hanging down to her left a little and snoring gently. The jingle of commercials would jolt her out of her sleep. Those weekday afternoons were pleasurable for me.

My parents were most disappointed when they realised in my early teens that I knew very little about the ancient Hindu epics, the Ramayana and the Mahabharata, but was well-acquainted with Hua Mulan, the brave Chinese warrior woman who disguised herself as a man. They found it quite exasperating when I asked for non-spicy food when we ate at Indian restaurants. The ultimate comfort food for me is still Cantonese: clear soup with tofu and salted mustard greens and a bowl of white rice, steamed to perfection with grains not too soft and slightly separated.

Before I started Primary One, my parents decided I should learn Chinese. A second language was, and still is, mandatory. In those early years of independence, there were three choices which catered to the main ethnic segments of Singapore's population – Chinese, Malay and Tamil, a dialect spoken in South India's Tamil Nadu from where the majority of Indian immigrants originated in the first hundred years of the founding of Singapore. As neither of my parents was from Tamil Nadu, Tamil was not an option.

Amah was keen for me to learn Chinese.

'By the time you are eight years old, you can write all my letters for me. You can read them too, as soon as the postman brings them to me.' She regularly paid an elderly Chinese man who wrote and read letters for illiterate immigrants. I had just started going with Amah at least once a fortnight to Chinatown; the letter reader-writer, an old man with a weather-beaten and kind face, fascinated me with his skills in calligraphy, turning simple strokes into elegant characters which combined to create a work of art on a piece of paper that was merely a medium to send news home. Every visit would be very sad, and Amah would cry; it always seemed to be bad news from home. When Amah cried, I cried too, even though I did not know why. She would not tell me. It just made me so sad to see her that way. Many years later I learnt her sadness was due to the unimaginable suffering brought upon her family, along with the rest of China, by the Cultural Revolution.

'I will pay you instead of Old Man San. We won't have to take the Number 12 bus to Chinatown just for that. Too far, too hot,' she said in halting Malay, excitedly. I shared in her excitement, wanting to help her and please her. I had no idea then that I would have to be at least twelve years old before I knew enough Chinese to write a simple letter to her family.

After much discussion and with Amah's opinion duly considered, my parents thought it might be best for me to take the path of least resistance. In the end, they chose Malay, a language that was easy to learn because it uses Romanised text. I will always be grateful for that decision. Being very similar to Bahasa Indonesia, my proficiency in Malay played a big part in helping me settle into village life in Bali forty years later.

When I was around ten, an American girl named Sue joined my Primary Five class. Sue was a novelty because of her blonde hair and blue eyes. She also asked a lot of questions, laughed a lot, and spoke more loudly than everyone else. She was like one of those girls I saw in those television shows from America – *The Brady Bunch* and *Partridge Family* – pretty, bubbly and talkative. She was very confident. I liked her instantly. I saw in her all I wanted to be but felt I wasn't. I did not like how she spoke, however. Half the time, I could not understand what she said. She used the 'd' sound for 't' in some words. She would say 'bedderrrr' instead of 'bet-tuh' for the word 'better'; she said 'can't' like the sound of the 'a' in 'hand' instead of the sound of 'a' in 'car'. She referred to sweets and chocolate as 'candy' which in Singapore is a coconut confection. In a matter of weeks, I got used to her accent and new American words, like when she said 'apartment' instead of 'flat' and 'elevator' instead of 'lift'. It was like watching an American show on television except without the Malay subtitles on which I relied heavily.

My early school years at Convent of the Holy Infant Jesus Opera Estate and later at Katong Convent were uneventful. The most dramatic moment for me was when Amah left to work in another household. I was twelve years old and missed her terribly. She continued to visit us nearly every Sunday for the next eight years until she made her final one-way trip to China but it took me a long time to get used to not having her around all the time.

A few months after Amah left, just before the Primary School Leaving Examinations, Sue returned to Ohio in America. She said her goodbyes without knowing if or when she would be back in Singapore again. Once she was gone, the classroom of nearly forty girls felt empty without her. I think most of us missed her, but no one more than I. All of us assumed we would never see her again.

Then, out of the blue one Sunday afternoon, she called and asked for me. When I said it was me, she delivered the most effusive 'hi' I had ever heard. I recognised the voice but was not sure. It seemed too good to be true. Sensing my hesitation, she said, 'It's Sue!'

'Sue!!!' I said, jumping around until I was entangled in the phone cord. 'Are you here on holiday? Gosh, how long has it been? A year?'

'About that, yeah. My parents moved back. My Dad got a job with Halliburton. I'm in an international school now. I lost my address book and did not have anyone's numbers. Imagine looking up all those Lees and Tans and Wongs in the directory. I sure as hell can't remember the Eurasian last names,' she said.

'Mine would be easy to find. Only two or three under Vas, I think.'

'That's what I thought. I could only remember two Indian names. There were too many under "Menon" to try but only two under "Vas". I tried the first Vas listed and you answered. Lucky *lah*!' She emphasised the *'lah'*. It was funny to hear Sue use the most ubiquitous of all Singlish words. I had never heard her say *lah* before and asked if she was making fun of me. She laughed.

'No! Don't be silly! I used it a lot for fun while I was back in the States and it just seems normal to use it here.' It was strange to think that a foreigner wanted to sound like me at a time when I was starting to imitate the girls on American television shows.

Sue came over the next weekend. It was a Saturday and we were having a late lunch in our poorly finished, sparsely furnished, government-subsidised apartment. My parents asked Sue to join us at the table. It was a simple Indian meal but Sue thought it was a grand spread.

'Man, this is so good! Do you eat like this every day or just on weekends?' she asked.

'Just weekends. But my mother made two extra dishes for you, the cauliflower and the spiced mutton,' I said and filled her plate with a second helping, noticing the chapatti pushed to one side of her plate.

'I prefer rice, thanks,' she said.

Soon, Sue came over more and more often, almost every weekend. She was the same pretty and lively girl but also a little different. I thought she was more boisterous, a lot cleverer and a lot more fun. I definitely wanted to be like Sue.

'Here, brought you some magazines. I've read them. Take your time. Just give them back when you're done,' she'd say, reaching into her big, yellow canvas bag and pulling out some glossy magazines.

There was always *Seventeen*, *Tiger Beat*, a couple of other magazines and sometimes her parents' *TIME* which accidentally found its way into the stack. She regularly brought audiotapes of American pop and rock music with her. I grew to like Kiss, Boston, BTO and Peter Frampton, musicians I had never heard of until I met Sue. We would just lie in my room and read or listen to music, usually both. We would also go to the beach near my home after dinner, when it was cooler.

I was fascinated by how much Sue knew about world events and quite intrigued that she even cared. I had no interest in what was happening around my own small country or the region, let alone the world.

'Hey, what do you think about that fastest plane in the world taking off? I thought it was far out! Conquered. Supersonic jet. Cool name for a plane, too. We talked about it in class today,' she said.

'Why do you say it like that, sounding like "Conquered"? It sounds weird. It's supposed to sound like "Cong-cord". That's how I've heard it being said,' I asked, wondering if it was yet another word the Americans said differently.

'I was thinking of the town in Massachusetts, Concord without the 'e' at the end. You're right, though, that's what they called it in school. Did you know the Concorde, as in "cong-cord", was made jointly by the British and French and was finished a few years ago? *Concorde* is the French spelling for "concord", an English word which means agreement,' she said, and noticed that I was now as interested as she was during her class discussion.

'No, I didn't know that. You're so clever! Where do you get all this information?' I asked.

'It's all over the papers and on the news! Big news!' she said, surprised at my ignorance.

I asked how her teacher ended up talking about a new, supersonic jet in class because in my school, teachers walked into the class, taught according to the syllabus, gave out homework and left. Most teachers did not like questions as they felt it was disruptive for a class of forty students.

'Some teachers tell us things, some ask questions but mostly it's the other way around. You won't get a discussion until you ask a question. It's not like you can't; I used to do it all the time when I was at your school,' she said.

I could not understand the concept of a discussion in a

classroom. When teachers asked a question, it was to test our knowledge or understanding of a subject. When students asked a question, which was extremely rare in my school, it was because we did not know or understand something. When a teacher spoke about something, it was always directly related to the syllabus. I could not remember a discussion in the classroom as Sue had just described.

'Don't you remember what it was like?' I asked, surprised she had forgotten. 'The teachers didn't like it. As soon as your hand went up, the teacher would say "Yes, Susan?" eyes rolling and in a tone that said you were a nuisance.'

'Yeah, I remember, all of them trying to intimidate me. I didn't care. It was their job to answer questions. Just try it. You'll never know,' Sue said. Soon after, I started raising my hand in class when I did not understand something, causing some teachers to write in my report book that I was a disruptive student. Wanting to be like Sue, I learnt not to care and expected answers.

It was because of Sue that I started to read beyond the newspaper headlines. Soon after I started to read *The Straits Times*, the main daily paper, I was able to discuss with genuine interest Anwar Sadat's visit to Israel and the worst air disaster in history at Tenerife and other major world events. It was my initiation into global citizenship. I felt clever and worldly wise. I was fourteen years old.

Sue was a voracious reader and encouraged me to borrow

her books.

'What? You're still reading Enid Blyton? Hello, you're already fourteen! Why would you still be interested in a group of girls in an English boarding school in the Fifties?' she asked. 'Why don't you pick up some books from my room when you visit next weekend? I just finished Hemingway's *The Old Man and The Sea*. Take that one, you'll like it. It's a good start,' she offered.

As I struggled with Wordsworth's 'I Wandered Lonely as a Cloud' in Secondary Two, Sue read Hemingway and Edgar Allan Poe. For pleasure, I should add. Sue gets all the credit for introducing me to the concept of reading to open my mind. It was those days when the foundations were laid for me to become a voracious reader in adulthood and a book club co-founder. She visited my school – her old school – several times a year when we had public events. We had sleepovers nearly every other week in each other's homes except during exams. She loved sleeping over at my home because we could easily sneak out and cross the highway to walk to the beach where we would smoke cigarettes, which Sue bought, and drink rum and coke or gin and lime which I took from my father's bar. I didn't like drinking as much as I liked smoking. I felt strong and grown-up just having that cigarette between my fingers. We smoked Marlboro and with images of cowboys on horses in my mind, it also made me feel American.

Through the few boring and sometimes difficult years of secondary school, there were a few girls at school whose company

I sought but it was always Sue who brightened up a bad day or week. It was Sue's encouragement and influence that helped me develop into the person I eventually became – confident, inquisitive, generous, socially conscious and an avid reader.

I was always skipping along the wide corridors in school, usually accompanied by a song in my head. I do not remember when the songs started, probably when I was about fifteen. There was a song for every emotion running through my mind from the highest highs to the lowest lows. Depending on how I was feeling, I would dig into the private collection buried in the recesses of my mind and pull out a song, sing to myself and bob my head along with the song. Sometimes I would play the same song for a few days in a row, like Simon and Garfunkel's '59th Bridge Song', telling me to slow down, I was moving too fast, I really had to make the morning last ... all the while looking for fun, loving life and feeling groovy. Very groovy.

When I was in Secondary Three, I cut some classes and went to the library. It wasn't so much that I was drawn to the library; I felt pushed away from the classroom. Most times I didn't feel the push but on the odd occasion when it came, I succumbed. It happened for all my lessons except literature. I adored my literature teacher, Ms Aileen Lau, the kindest and the only inspiring teacher I ever had in all my years in school. The teacher of some other classes I skipped would send the class monitor to look for me and each time the teacher would ask why and each time I would just shrug my shoulders. Fearing suspension or even expulsion, I did not know how to tell the teacher I was bored and did not want to be in her class. The teachers eventually came to accept it as part of my behaviour and went through the motions of hauling me back to class on those days when I disappeared to the library.

When I started Secondary Four, my last year at Katong Convent, I started to feel that everyone around me, even my teachers, were slow. Frustratingly slow. Like I was cycling at a normal speed and they were behind, not even trying to catch up. I didn't have this feeling all the time but it was for long enough to notice. Everyone had to work hard for a major rite of passage exam at the end of the year, the dreaded General Certificate of Education Ordinary Levels, better known as O-levels. My entire future was going to be determined by how well or badly I did in these exams; teachers sometimes warned us that failing them meant working as a sales assistant at a department store while passing with good grades meant going on to pre-university for two years and sitting the GCE Advanced or A-levels, doing well enough to secure a place in university. I had trouble focusing and my grades dived but I felt quick and smart in my head. School was boring. I hung out with a few people, all very nice girls and fun to be with, during recess and sometimes after school too, but Sue had been my best friend for over three years now so I didn't actually have any really close friends in my school. I liked many of them, but I had started to feel different from them. I did not know why; it was just the feeling of a perceptive, sensitive sixteen-year-old.

Some teachers told me that I was too wild, a little crazy and needed to tone it down. Wild? Crazy? And tone exactly *what* down? They liked the word 'crazy' and used it with contempt. Looking back, I am sure if they had they used the word 'crazy' with a little wonderment it might have softened the delivery. I did not think I was wild. I drank and I smoked cigarettes, but only with Sue, and mainly at the beach near my home. There were girls in my school as young as thirteen who were sleeping with their boyfriends, usually from St. Patrick's next door. To me that was wild. I didn't even have a boyfriend.

Early into Secondary Four, I cut my uniform pinafore. It was so short that when I walked down the corridor in the direction of a classroom where a notoriously strict teacher, Madam Tan, happened to be teaching because the usual teacher was sick, she yelled out my name and asked me to step into her classroom. She removed her ugly black butterfly-rimmed glasses, looked at me from top to toe and said that tutus were not part of the school uniform. The whole class laughed.

'Your O-levels are months away. At the rate you are going, Ms Vas, you will fail all your exams and end up leading a life of nothingness,' Madam Tan continued without trying to hide her contempt. 'Nothingness. Mark my words,' she stressed.

While wondering if 'nothingness' was a correct word, I had

this urge to pull her big, unnaturally fluffy hair to see if it was a wig. Thankfully she asked me to get out before I could lift my arm. She knew she could not make me buy a new pinafore because it was the last year of school. A week later, I used indelible red ink to draw daisies – because they were Sue's favourite flowers – on the mandatory white canvas shoes we had to wear as part of our school uniform. I must have been very self-absorbed; it never occurred to me that in a school which was strict about uniforms and did not allow the use of jewellery other than a watch or a Catholic medallion; where hair ties had to be in blue, black or white and prefects – fellow students selected by teachers and given authority to enforce school rules – went around checking the length of our pinafores; where shoes and socks had to be as white as our bleached blouses, well, of course bright red daisies on filthy canvas shoes were going to be as conspicuous as flowers growing in the Sahara. Of course the prefects would have a field day booking me for detention. It was not long before I had to white wash my shoes every other day, instead of once a week, to keep those red daisies covered.

Where most Catholic and even some non-Catholic girls used laminated pictures of The Virgin Mary or Our Lady of Fatima as bookmarks in their textbooks, I had flimsy cut-outs of Peter Frampton whom I thought to be the most beautiful man in the world. Sue took them off some of her magazines and gave them to me. I particularly liked the picture taken off his album *Frampton*

Comes Alive. I habitually kissed this picture every time I saw it. Once I had the misfortune of sitting barely a foot from one of my teachers, on a day when I opened my book, saw the picture, smiled widely, picked it up with both hands, kissed it and whispered 'You are the greatest!'

Mrs Hu, a teacher I never liked, witnessed all this, looked at me with an intense loathing and said, 'You really are mad.' I think I just smiled which riled her more and she promptly sent me out to 'reflect on my actions'. I was happy for the solitude. I reflected on why Singapore didn't have boys who looked like Peter Frampton. I thought maybe one day I might marry him. It was a most pleasurable thought.

Madam Tan, the teacher who called my short pinafore a tutu and told me I was going to live a life of nothingness, also told me a few months later that she could see the devil in my eyes. She said it with some kindness in her voice, but the words were so harsh I could not know if she was telling me the truth or just being wicked. I wondered if it was true. Several weeks later, Madam Tan stopped me in the corridor, made me spit out my chewing gum and said, 'It must be your friend's influence. Just remember, you are not American, you know.'

After my O-levels, I left Katong Convent for a two-year pre-university course in another school. I found my first boyfriend, Vishal, who dumped me within months but we remained good friends. Soon after, I became friends with two other girls who now live in San Francisco and remain amongst my closest friends. I had a great time with them after school during the week and with Sue on weekends. Sometimes Sue joined us after school if she did not have much homework on a Thursday or Friday afternoon. We smoked a little, drank a little and, using portable audio tape players, listened to rock music introduced by Sue. We had our own little secret garden.

Amah was by now in her mid-sixties and working part-time to save up for her final trip to China. During her regular weekly visits, Amah would gently tell me every now and then that I was changing too quickly. I would take her hands in mine and tell her I was not a child any more. Then one day, while Amah was visiting, I had an argument with my mother about wearing the clothes Sue had given me. My mother thought the skin-tight denim jeans and skimpy top were too indecent and – her exact words – low-class.

'Did you just say "low-class"? Like we are so high-class? Mummy, all my friends, including Sue, are in a higher class than me. If you want to talk about high-class or low-class, we are low-class people who pretend to be high-class. We are not even middle-class like all our neighbours.' I was very angry at my mother for suggesting Sue was low-class because of her clothes.

Amah, with a sad voice I had not heard in years, chimed in and said I was becoming like that white girl, not a good girl, she is a bad influence. She tearfully told me that I must not be American like that white girl.

'You must not forget your roots. All children must respect their elders. You cannot argue with your mother. You are still a child. You cannot raise your voice like that,' Amah said, tears welling in her eyes. Her Malay had improved over the years. 'Good girls do not behave like that. They don't talk so much, don't show off how clever they are. They do not wear such tight clothes and T-shirts with so little material which show so much skin. Very bad way to dress. Must not be American,' Amah said. She pulled out her handkerchief and dabbed her eyes while shaking her head to register her disapproval. 'Must not be American' sounded so racist to my newly opened, still-developing yet opinionated mind.

'You two are terrible! As bad as the white racists, thinking that your race is superior. Ha! Being part of a civilisation going back thousands of years does not make you superior. Why harp on it? I feel Indian, I feel Chinese but I also feel American. If you wanted to be traditional, you should have stayed in your backward villages and lived like ostriches with your heads buried in the ground. You are pathetic. Leave me alone!' I screamed at my mother and Amah, tore up a magazine that was on the table and stormed out the door. While on the bus going into town, I thought about Amah dabbing her eyes and I started to cry. I could not understand what possessed me to lash out the way I did. I said a Sanskrit mantra and promised myself I would be good. I would not make Amah cry ever again.

That night, Amah, who was so troubled by my response that

she waited for me to come home, sat in my room and gently told me she cared deeply for me and wanted to help me.

'Maybe you have bad spirits inside you. Or maybe too much heaty food, not enough *yin*. Your mother will make more cooling food for you from tomorrow. Carrots, cucumber, tofu. Even watermelon. Try for a few weeks. You will get better. Don't worry, no need to go to temple,' Amah said as she massaged my arm.

'Temple? Why, Amah? You actually want a temple medium to exorcise me? You can't be serious!' I said and knew right away by the look on her face that she was serious.

'I cared for you for twelve years, from the time you were born. You are like my child. I know something is wrong with you but I don't know what. Your daddy has the same thing but your mummy doesn't know what to do. I can't tell her what to do but for me, you are different. You have my heart,' said Amah. 'I'm afraid you have spirits inside and the only cure is to drive them out of your body. But let us hope it is just your diet. All that spicy Indian food and mutton for a child raised on Cantonese-style vegetables and fish is not good for your system. Some Indian people can manage, you cannot. You are my Chinese girl,' she said. Listening to her gentle voice and looking at her soft face while remembering the events of that afternoon, I believed for a moment that I might actually be possessed by spirits.

'No!' I said as I pulled my arm away from Amah's soft hands. 'No! I am not possessed. Maybe my diet needs to change but there is nothing wrong with me.' I began to cry. Amah held my hand. 'I just need to control my temper. I will try my best to be good Amah, I promise. I won't shout at anyone, especially Mummy and I won't shout at you again.' I held back my tears as I made that promise. 'Sue never shouts at people. She is good to her mother. She makes me happy. She makes me forget all that is bad about Daddy and living in this horrible flat. She helped me get through my years in Katong Convent.'

After two weeks on a diet of cooling *yin* foods prepared without spices or fat, I seemed better. I ate a lot of yogurt and cucumber and drank at least two large glasses of barley water every day. I did not lose my temper for several months.

* * *

So who was I? Indian in spirit and demeanour, Chinese in affinity? A Chinese trapped in an Indian body? Was I neither Indian nor Chinese or maybe both in equal measure? Maybe a failed Asian and a pretend American, a fake? Or was it possible to just be plain no-racial-classification me, sometimes with a huge spring in my step and other times with a bad, uncontrollable temper?

At eighteen, I wasn't sure who I was, but if being who I was at the time made me American, then that's what I wanted to be. It made me feel free and natural. I no longer had to try to blend in, to submit to other people's expectations of how a teenage Asian girl should be. I found myself torn between the two most influential and important people in my life. I adored Amah and wanted her to be proud of me, but I also wanted to feel free, just like Sue. I wanted to learn to control my temper but I did not want to have to tone anything else down.

All I knew was that I wanted to be me without being bad.

CHAPTER 2

'Experience, travel – these are as education in themselves.'

Euripides

At nineteen, I became a flight stewardess with Singapore Airlines, consistently ranked amongst the world's best airlines. The job happened by chance. My parents were dead against it so I had to apply for it in secret.

The plan was for me to go to university after which my parents intended to marry me off to a suitable boy, as was the practice amongst their community in those days. Extended family homes being quite commonplace then, Indian parents preferred brides and grooms from the same community for their children. That was over and above the usual list of demands which included 'university educated, light-skinned, good job and good family'. I did not mind the arranged marriage that much but I did badly in my exams so a university education in Singapore was out of the question. My parents were beginning to think about making me work in my father's struggling real estate business. I could not bear the thought of working with my temperamental father whose assistants and agents routinely left after a few months.

A family friend who visited one afternoon suggested I join Singapore Airlines as a stewardess. The national airline was expanding rapidly and had some exciting routes. Mrs Dani's husband had just joined the airline as a pilot and the family had moved from India. Mrs Dani thought a few years flying around the world was a great idea; so did I. My mother obviously thought otherwise. After Mrs Dani left, my mother told me pointedly I was not to become a stewardess as such a 'low-class' job would bring shame to the family. That word again. In economic terms, we were probably a lower middle-class family; I could not see how an honest job could bring shame. It was an inane comment quite typical of my mother. In the first five minutes of the suggestion being made that afternoon, I had made up my mind. I was going to be a stewardess and if that meant being kicked out of the house, then all the better.

'They're just waitresses. Much worse, in fact. They clean toilets. I've heard some of the girls sleep with pilots and passengers. No daughter of mine will be allowed to take on such a lowly job. If you dare become a stewardess, I will kick you out of the house but not before giving you a proper thrashing,' my father said when I raised the idea during dinner that evening. My mother, younger sister, Rita, and I were silent. My father promptly shunned my older sister when she left the unholy atmosphere of our home as soon as she turned twenty-one just months before to escape years of physical and mental abuse by him.

To me, there was no appeal in living in a flat with parents who were narrow-minded and bickered constantly. The thought of marriage as being the only way out of the house, which it was then, was too desperate. On top of that, my father was unpredictable and lost his temper over the most trivial matter while my mother escaped into a world of spirituality, joining a few groups of friends for Hindu fellowship, chanting Sanskrit mantras and hymns a few times a week. My father rarely hit me or my younger sister but when he did, it hurt whether it was a slap or whip. Even then, I imagined that a 'proper thrashing' seemed like a small price to pay to get out of the house.

* * *

After going for three interviews while pretending to my parents that I was looking for temporary office jobs, I signed on the dotted line with Singapore Airlines. I was all set to see the world. I was going to make it my oyster. While telling my parents about my new job, expecting to be evicted that night, I mentioned the heavily discounted flights they could enjoy and they immediately became more supportive of my decision. I was not thrown out of the house.

I was very proud of my career choice. Singapore Airlines was then and still remains the world's most awarded airline, largely due to the in-flight service delivered by the iconic Singapore Girl, that girl-woman in her figure-hugging Balmain-designed sarong kebaya, dolled up with blue eye-shadow and traffic-stopping red lipstick with matching fingernails. The Singapore Girl was much more than just a flight stewardess or trolley dolly. She was, and still is, a constant part of a solid marketing strategy dreamed up by a Western advertising man with a vision. The marketing pitch worked. My pride and joy was not about being a stewardess; it was all about being a 'Singapore Girl, You're A Great Way To Fly'.

During my three-month training course, Amah decided it was the right time to return to China for good. I saw her the night before her ship set sail for Guangdong in Southern China. We just sat in her room, not speaking a word until I had to leave an hour later.

'You will really write to me? You will try to see me in China? If it is too difficult, don't trouble yourself, my dear child. I will think of you every day and tell my children and grandchildren stories about you,' Amah said.

'I promise, Amah. I will go to Old Man San or ask my Chinese friends for help to write my letters and to read yours. I will see you soon. Have a safe journey, Amah,' I said. I gave her a hug. I caught a whiff of that familiar scent of starch on her blouse, which zipped me back to my earliest memory. I wept on the bus all the way home.

I could not wait to start flying so I could see Amah. I also wanted to see Sue who was already in her second year of university in Ohio. As Singapore Airlines neither flew to Guangzhou in those days nor to Ohio, I needed to earn annual leave and save up for airfare and spending money on those trips.

In no time, I was ready for my first flight as a trainee stewardess. I was so excited that I hardly slept the night before. I went to Hong Kong and had a one-night layover. It was my first time in Hong Kong and I disliked it intensely the moment the crew bus left Kai Tak airport – the ugliness of Kowloon with its filthy, decrepit buildings and the room at the Miramar Hotel with its bright white neon lights, drab furnishings, depressing pictures on the wall and the lingering mustiness. Within an hour of checking in, I went for a wander on my own and found that everyone spoke Cantonese. I saw two old hunch-backed women near a street corner chatting and clumsily piling flattened cardboard boxes wearing *samfoos*, a tunic and loose pants, like Amah used to wear. Overwhelmed by this sense of homecoming through the familiarity of my first spoken language and the pitiful sight of the old women, I leaned against a wall and reached into my wallet for a picture of Amah I have carried since I was twelve.

Memories of Amah came flooding back and I began to cry. She was probably a three-hour drive north, yet I could not see her because in those days my Singapore passport strictly forbade travel to all communist countries, including China. I had heard that bribes could get me a return passage across the border but I did not want to risk jail or a sacking. She was so close and yet so far. *Someday, Amah, I will come and see you.*

I felt too weak to wander and headed back to the hotel. There was a McDonald's on the way. Feeling slightly hungry, I stopped to get a strawberry sundae. I sat by a huge window and looked out onto a narrow lane filled with shops and people who seemed to be in a hurry. I finished the sundae and walked back feeling much better. It was the first time I became aware of the soothing effects of ice cream on my sad mind.

Barely a week after my first flight, I was on my way to Copenhagen. It was July, just the beginning of the summer tourist season. My first day in Copenhagen had me thinking I had died and gone to heaven. It was an eight-hour flight from Bahrain where we had stopped for the night. Everyone was tired. Actually, I could see they were tired from the moment we met at the lobby in Bahrain for our pick-up at some witching hour – probably somewhere between two and four in the morning. I, on the other hand, remember being so restless that someone asked if I was okay. 'Yes, yes, I'm just so excited!' I said, almost squealing.

I had picked up some brochures from the Danish consular office in Singapore before the flight. I had read Hans Christian Andersen's fairy tales when I was young and *The Little Mermaid* was my favourite book. I wanted to see the famous statue of the little mermaid sitting on a rock in the harbour. I could not wait to go to Tivoli, an amusement park the Danish used to call a pleasure garden. Then there was Kronborg, the fifteenth-century castle that Shakespeare used as a setting for Hamlet, his longest play and one of the most powerful tragedies in English literature. I also wanted to walk down the charming Strøget, Denmark's famous pedestrian street with its little shops housed in beautiful Scandic buildings dating as far back as the seventeenth century. There was so much to do and so little time. I aligned myself with a few really nice crew members and hung out with them. I quickly learnt that many of the cabin crew were inclined to sleep for hours and hours at a stretch and had strange sleeping patterns due to the time difference, sleeping during the day and partying or playing *mahjong* and card games into the wee hours of the morning.

In my moment of naiveté, probably a result of my youthful enthusiasm, I swore I would spend every available waking moment exploring every city I visited – the people, the culture, the food, the sights and sounds and smells. I felt very energetic, needed very little sleep and couldn't understand the listlessness of the crew that surrounded me.

Three months after my first flight to Copenhagen, I was on my way there again. I had turned twenty just three days earlier. I had been ill on my birthday and felt progressively worse. The doctor said it was stomach flu and I should just rest. He gave me a medical certificate for my flight but I did not want it. Something inside me desperately felt the need to go to Copenhagen that night. I decided I was well enough, packed for an eight-day trip and took a long pre-flight nap. I was nineteen on my previous trip. I was now twenty. It was to be my personal new year and new decade, full of new beginnings.

On that flight to Copenhagen, a young pilot did his rounds in the cabin and introduced himself to the crew in the various galleys. I shook his hand, we spoke a few words and he left. In five minutes, I was totally smitten with this co-pilot, Bob.

In Bahrain the next morning, while I was sunning my sallow skin, Bob came by my pool chair to say hello. I was thinking, all these stewardesses lying around half naked and he comes and says hello to *me*. I felt like a teenager in love. After all, I was still a teenager up until a few days before. He left soon after to join the captain in the air-conditioned pool bar.

I could not stop thinking of Bob. I lay awake at night wondering what he was doing. Was he watching television or reading a book? Did he order room service or did he have his dinner at the hotel café? Did he think of me, even for a few seconds?

We arrived in Copenhagen the next day. While waiting for our luggage at the airport, I looked up to see the pilots and engineer making their way down the escalator. Bob looked so handsome in his uniform with the Senior First Officer's three gold bars.

'One day, I will marry Bob,' I told one of the stewardesses standing next to me by the luggage belt. That was in October 1982.

'You're mad. You hardly know him. You've only just started flying. Lots of eligible guys out there. Don't marry crew, you'll only end up in heartbreak hotel,' she warned. I later learnt her husband was a steward who had cheated on her repeatedly.

You're mad. First time in a long time someone had called me that. I resented being called mad for my instinct or for just dreaming big.

Early the next morning, I went along with some crew on an excursion to Malmo in Sweden. I asked Bob if he wanted to come along but he'd been to Malmo before and preferred to stay in Copenhagen and do his own thing.

When we returned from Sweden that evening, I decided that time was running out; I would soon be in Singapore and Bob would probably meet someone on his next flight. Or maybe he already had a girlfriend; why did I not think of that? Anyway, if I wanted to marry him, I needed to at least make sure there was no girlfriend and then give him a reason to see me in Singapore. It was nearly eight o'clock at night and he was not in his room. Probably out for dinner, either alone or with the captain. I slipped a note under his door and asked him to call me. Less than an hour later, he called. In my head, I heard a song and it was Lou Reed asking me to take a walk on the wild side and something about coloured girls going doo doo doo doo doo doo ... Like the coloured girl I was, I did.

So I put on my tiny red shorts and a skimpy top, sprayed

Chanel No 5 around my neck and on my arms and took the lift up to the seventh floor and knocked on his door.

'Big room. Better suited to the Scandinavians,' I said, looking around, taking in the two single beds, the bedside table, the carpet, all very different from my tiny room with its narrow single bed.

'Yes, it is rather a big room. I don't see how they can build such tiny single rooms like the one you have,' he replied, suddenly aware that I was wondering how he knew about our tiny rooms. Did he have a pleasurable encounter with a stewardess on one of his previous flights?

'Nice view,' I said quickly, looking out the window. It was nearly ten o'clock at night and the street lights were shining brightly. It looked cold outside.

My stomach felt a little queasy and I did not know what else to say. I started to think maybe this was a mistake. I contemplated leaving and just as I had decided to do so, Bob came over and looked out the window with me. Before I knew it, I was consumed by very active hormones, turned around and very happily and shamelessly kissed him. Seconds later, I just as shamelessly removed my clothes. I was actually very nervous, but pretended I had done this before. Within moments, I had to confess this was all new to me and could he please be very gentle. Much of that evening remains a blur but I do remember thinking that I was glad to finally be rid of my virginity and that I wanted to be with Bob. An arranged marriage was no longer an option. Not only was I insufficiently educated, I was no longer a virgin and had allowed myself to be dishonoured by a non-Indian man ten years older. I was too happy to care.

A few months after Bob and I started dating, I went to Ohio to see Sue. We spent a glorious week together.

'So, when will you be back? It would be nice if you came to my graduation. You've got two years to save up for that,' she said. 'My parents are moving back this summer so I won't be going to Singapore for a very long time.'

'I don't know, Sue. I get discount travel up to the West Coast but still with that cost and the flight to Ohio, it all adds up. It's not like I get a lot of time off either and I want to go on holidays with Bob. He loves to go to Europe. I want to marry him and holidays together will help make him want to marry me,' I said. We both knew that distance and the high cost of travel meant that neither of us would be flying out to see each other for a very long time and promised to stay in touch by writing often. That was when we both knew we would always be best friends, no matter how many miles and time zones separated us.

* * *

Less than a year after I had become a stewardess, before I turned twenty-one, I had flown to nearly twenty cities in North Asia, Europe, the Middle East, Australia and the United States. I was a self-styled intrepid traveller, foregoing shopping for sightseeing. I functioned like that Energiser bunny that just keeps going and going, extremely energetic and often, I am sure, every bit as irritating to those around me.

By now, after a year of dating in between our unforgiving schedules which often had us on opposite ends of the world, I had fallen truly-madly-deeply in love with Bob and had a lot of sex to make up for a late start. So sure that I would marry him, I signed up for a two-year correspondence course for a diploma in Early Childhood Education at the London Montessori Centre. I figured this was the perfect job for a pilot's wife, allowing me a little independence and pocket money with enough time at home to care for my husband and future brood.

I loved travelling as a stewardess, staying in good hotels, usually a Hilton or Sheraton, and having a few nice crew members with whom I shopped, dined and explored various cities. Some crew were exceptional, making a fifteen-day flight seem like a short vacation. I loved certain cities for their soul, for the life they seemed to breathe into themselves – Cairo, Paris, Sydney, London, San Francisco. Sue's influence stayed with me; I read at least three books a month, mostly fiction, and kept up with world events by reading the *International Herald Tribune* and the *Wall Street Journal* during long flights.

I loved wearing the Singapore Airlines uniform. It made me feel elegant and beautiful. I was always aware of people stopping to look when we arrived or left as a group at airports and in hotel lobbies. I distinctly remember in the late Eighties, when going down the escalator at Los Angeles Airport, a stewardess excitedly said 'Curiosity killed the cat, look, curiosity killed the cat!' while looking down to her left, waving. Apparently, that was the name of a popular boy band. The young men in that troupe were already standing in line at the immigration counter, and looking up at us stewardesses making our way down. They looked and they smiled and although I smiled back I didn't care because I had no idea who they were. People looked at us that way all the time. I felt so proud to be a Singapore Girl although the reality also meant dirty work like cleaning the cabin lavatories. It was not glamorous; the glamour was extinguished as soon as the seat belt sign was switched off and the work began. But it was great fun.

I was on a high. I remember that feeling; distinct yet indescribable, the feeling of wanting to fly. I felt it but I had no idea what it was or why it was happening. It had happened before but not with the same intensity. I could not understand my friends who said they really enjoyed flying but seemed so unenthusiastic about sightseeing or needed so much sleep. I was astounded by the number of cabin crew I had flown with who had visited so many beautiful European cities and had never taken what those places had to offer – the museums, the churches, the walks along rivers and lanes that held so much history. Thankfully, there were enough people who were as interested as I was so I did not always have to go exploring on my own. I loved the experiences flying gave me. I could handle the body clock issues and I was ready for more. In fact, I just couldn't get enough.

* * *

Barely two years after I had become a stewardess, I returned home from a flight in the early afternoon and found my sister, Rita, at home when she should have been in school. When she turned her face to say hello to me, I was horrified to see her left eye swollen, almost entirely closed and a large patch in the ugliest shades of blue, red and purple. She could not possibly go to school looking like that. Apparently, my father had lost his temper about something trivial and picked up one of our dining chairs with the intention of hitting my mother. I never liked those chairs; they were very heavy, uncomfortable and quite badly made. Hitting my mother who was only four feet eleven inches with a heavy chair and the brute force my fat father possessed could have killed her. When Rita stepped in to protect my mother, my father punched her. She was only fourteen.

They saved themselves from more harm by running into Rita's bedroom, locking the door and staying there until my father left for work the next morning. As soon as I learnt what had happened, I decided we had to go to the police. We needed to take out a Personal Protection Order, which would prevent my father from coming within thirty feet of my mother. My mother was dead against the idea. She wanted to keep our dirty secrets within the family. She was concerned about finances and what her friends would say. I assured her I could support the family on my salary. She could not see that she also needed to protect herself and Rita from an abusive relationship. My mother seemed oblivious to any danger while I had a real fear that I could be away on a flight to some city and getting a call from Singapore Airlines telling me I needed to get home urgently as my mother or sister or both had been killed.

When my mother realised I was going to the police with Rita anyway, she came along. The police took one look at my sister, got us to make a report, issued a restraining order immediately and asked us to change the locks. They were going to call my father at the office to tell him that he was not allowed to go home that day. My mother asked them not to. She wanted my father to come home for dinner and for me to break the news. Although she was putting me in the line of fire, I agreed. After dinner, my mother and sister quickly washed the dishes and locked themselves in my bedroom where there was a phone. I was quite sure I would die that night. If my father could try and hit my mother's tiny frame with a heavy chair for a silly housekeeping matter, then what chance did I have for telling him that he had to leave his home? To this day, I do not know what I was thinking when I agreed to tell my father about the restraining order. Knowing my father's temper and his inclination for violence, it was suicidal to tell him face to face about the police report and his legal obligation to leave the flat.

As was his usual routine after dinner, my father planted himself in front of the television. Trembling, with a copy of the restraining order in my hand, I sat diagonally across from him on the sofa. I do not know why but at that moment my mind scanned the living room for pictures, lamps and the Indian ornaments that decorated the place. All I could think at the time was that it was an ugly room. I was probably going to be strangled or thrown out of the window ten floors to my death from this ugly living room. I started slowly and quietly, terrified but trying to remain calm.

'Ummmm, Daddy. I was very upset to see Rita's eye like that. She told me what happened. I am shocked you would try such a thing on Mummy and then take it out on Rita,' I said as I tried unsuccessfully to tame my quivering voice

'She got in the way. I'm lord of this house. You are nobody to question me,' he replied in a gruff voice. His eyes were on the television screen.

His response made me more scared but at the same time it strengthened my resolve to let this bully know that the game was over. I genuinely believed my father would try to kill me and wondered if I should just let the police do their job the next day, while he was at work.

'You may be the lord of this house but you cannot be abusive to Mummy or to Rita. We made a police report today and got a restraining order. We were not supposed to let you come home this evening but Mummy told the police she wanted me to be the one to tell you,' I said, realising I had spoken very quickly and had moved to the edge of my seat.

'Who the hell do you think you are? Nothing but a lowly prostitute in a uniform serving beer to drunks,' he boomed, while he pointed and violently shook his finger at me. He continued, 'I am lord of this house! Understand? You are nothing and nobody. I swear I will kill you before I leave,' he was screaming, his eyes bloodshot and bulging.

Just as he said the last few words 'before I leave', I saw him moving in his seat. I jumped off the sofa and ran to my room, where I had recently installed a phone, warning him as I ran that I would call the police if he tried anything. My sister heard me and quickly opened the door. As I rushed in, I banged it shut and locked it behind me. My back against the door, I slid to the floor and sobbed with relief now that I was safe. Being grossly overweight and pot-bellied, my father could not spring out of his chair quickly enough. He had to struggle and it took several seconds longer to get his porcine self out of the soft-cushioned seat into which he had comfortably sunk, prepared to be entertained for two hours of *Magnum PI* and *Solid Gold*. It was those precious seconds that saved me.

The next morning we waited until after nine o'clock before

quietly opening the door. He had left. We got the locks changed within an hour and sent a note to him at the office that the locks had been changed and that he would be arrested if he came home. I offered to pack his clothes and send them to him. Our home was peaceful and completely devoid of fear. It took my mother some time to adjust. Given her traditional Indian upbringing she was more concerned about what her friends would say.

'In two weeks, Daddy and I would have been married twenty-five years. I know you would say there was nothing to celebrate but still, twenty-five years of marriage, good or bad, is still a long time,' said my mother. I think initially my mother preferred being an abused wife than a separated one.

It was April 1984. I was twenty-one and overnight became head of a small household. My mother was in her early fifties and my sister who had just turned fifteen were now entirely dependent on me. My mother had less than a hundred dollars in the bank. We were not expecting my father to send us any money so I had to dig into my small savings and start being more frugal.

'I am sorry to be such a burden on you, Mahita. It won't be long before our papers are processed and Rita and I will be off to America. I'll sell this flat and use the money to get us started until I find a job,' my mother said that morning when we felt completely free for the first time in years. 'America has very good programmes for immigrants. They even give us training for some jobs.'

'Don't worry, Mummy. I will take care of you and Rita for as long as it takes. Once you leave, I'll rent a place in Bedok or Tampines, near the airport,' I said. I did not tell her I planned to move in with Bob who had asked me to live with him. I told him that living with a man before marriage was unthinkable in the Indian community and would bring undeserved shame upon my mother. Now that she was leaving, however, I did not think it would matter but had to wait until she left for America.

From the next flight thereafter, I became more thrifty and exercised restraint when I accompanied fellow crew on their shopping jaunts in Amsterdam, Hong Kong, London, Paris and Tokyo. I saved more than half of my salary which went to my mother every month for household expenses. I knew of countless other stewardesses who did the same, many even saving to put a sibling through university. Despite the reduction in my personal spending, I still enjoyed flying. Bob was very generous on our holidays, paying for everything.

* * *

Often enough, I found myself pushed by an inner energy during those long never-ending night flights when passengers were asleep or watching a movie which at that time was projected on the bulkhead. I would virtually walk all the way to the cities I visited. For instance, on an evening take-off at around 9 p.m.

in Singapore, headed for Melbourne or Dubai, landing about seven hours later, I would happily walk up and down the aisles, constantly asking passengers if they would like another drink. In Economy Class, most crew would simply clear an empty cup. To them, if a passenger wanted another drink, he could jolly well ask for one. I, on the other hand, always offered a drink as I cleared an empty cup. To me, it was basic courtesy but I also needed to keep myself busy. Besides, it was also the standard set by some senior crew I respected. Many passengers found it hard to refuse free alcoholic beverages. In all the years I flew, I must have served enough beers to match any Oktoberfest maid in all of Germany and enough gin and tonics to quench the thirst of every British officer's thirst in the days of the Raj.

I unabashedly flirted with some passengers, usually in First or Business Class because there were fewer passengers and service was more personalised. I never meant anything by it, just some harmless fun. I took the flirting up a notch and made it a game when passengers readily handed out their cards with the suggestion that I call them when I was next in Sydney or San Francisco or wherever. It very quickly became an ego trip. The passengers with whom I tended to flirt were all British, Australian or American. There were some attractive Asian passengers but none seemed interested in me. I think I scared them away. As for the men from Continental Europe, the Gunthers, Pierres and Giovannis, I just didn't give them a chance. They may have been smarter and funnier than the John Smiths but I found it hard to break the ice during the meal service. I figured if I didn't get their attention by then, I wasn't going to succeed in the next six or twelve hours. There were a lot of name cards collected over the years, most of which were left on the galley counter top. For me, the game ended just before touchdown, soon after which passengers disembarked and became a distant memory, including those delightful passengers who were so generous with their time and expressions of desire during the flight. Years later when I read these words in Dr Kay Redfield Jamison's seminal book, *An Unquiet Mind: A Memoir of Moods and Madness*, I knew exactly what she meant. I had been there many, many times before:

'Sensuality is pervasive and the desire to seduce and be seduced irresistible. Feelings of ease, intensity, power, well-being, financial omnipotence, and euphoria pervade one's marrow.'

I found myself talking non-stop on the bus ride from the airport to the hotel when everyone just wanted to sleep. No one ever asked me to shut up so I didn't, oblivious to the annoyance I must have caused. After checking-in, most crew, even the young and very junior crew, slept for hours on end but I didn't need much sleep. I would spend my time reading or watching television and, as long as the city was safe, I would go out for a walk all by myself.

Sometimes I felt very sad when I had no reason to be. It was an unusual sadness, as if my heart was broken and bleeding into a bottomless well. Yet there was nothing to cause such heartbreak. Sometimes I would cry for nothing. Other times, there would be an emptiness I found hard to understand, let alone explain. For about ten days at a stretch I would feel tired and irritable even though I'd had enough sleep. There were days when I just would not, could not, summon the energy to leave my bed to go and shower. There were two more modules for my Montessori diploma course for which I just could not bring myself to do the research properly and ended up handing in what I thought was mediocre work. By the time I was done with the course, I received a Distinction and can only guess that I must have written exceptionally well in the first four modules. Thankfully, these moments did not happen very frequently, maybe once or twice a year, and did not last very long. I usually forgot about them.

There were times when I thought about death. I wondered about it from the top of the Eiffel Tower on my first visit to Paris one cold and dreary February. I couldn't have been the only one because I noticed it was all fenced up at the top and there was no other reason for that but to prevent people like me from doing what we think is the right thing at the right time. Sometimes it became an obsession especially when I stayed at high-rise hotels with sliding doors, which opened onto balconies. The Ala Moana Hotel in Honolulu was one such hotel and I distinctly remember one day when I got a room that was above the hotel pool. I thought aloud, 'Oh if I decide to jump off this balcony, the pool will save me.' The fact that it was not normal to think about jumping fifteen floors and having a swimming pool save me simply did not cross my mind. I only remember this because I had shared a room with a fellow crew member and she heard me. She looked at me and said, 'You're really crazy.' For a moment there, I thought I might be, but I dismissed it as her just being different and candid.

On one of those flights, I found myself in London. It was a particularly cold and grey winter. I spent most of my three days in bed. I had flown with one of the crew members before and, as we got on so well, we asked for connecting rooms at the hotel. Like many of the other crew, she loved London for the shopping. So did I.

'What's wrong with you? You seemed fine in Dubai and on the flight to London,' she asked. 'What happened to all that shopping you wanted to do? *Char siew fan* at Bayswater? Your favourite musical, *Fiddler On The Roof*? One moment so excited, now so dead. Aiyoh!'

'Nothing's wrong. Just very tired. Must be all those months of sightseeing, shopping and our cruel working hours that are catching up with me.' I tried to believe this even as I felt hollow and empty inside. A feeling so flat, so lifeless, it did not even warrant a description. I was not only too tired; I had lost all interest in shopping, not even to go to The Body Shop which in the early Eighties was on most stewardesses' must-do list. I was all set to stand in line and pay scalper's rates for a ticket to watch Topol as the Fiddler. That day, all I wanted to do was sleep. Actually, I really wanted to sleep and never wake up. I wanted to die but I did not say anything.

'Then rest, I'll bring you dinner and buy some sandwiches or fruit for lunch tomorrow. I'll also buy some snacks. See how you feel after that.' She ended up getting me all my meals and left me to get as much sleep as I needed. I was very grateful for her care and thanked her profusely as I reimbursed her for all my meals and snacks.

I did not feel any better on our last day in London.

'I think you should see a doctor now, or right after breakfast. It's eight o'clock and we are flying out tonight. Trust me, you are in no shape to work,' she said. 'Going on-board like this makes it harder for the rest of us. You'll be useless. Call a doctor, get an M.C. and let a standby crew take your place.'

I saw the doctor and with great reluctance took my first medical certificate – that dreaded M.C. – which now prevented me from having a spotless attendance record – and flew back to Singapore as a passenger. When I reached home, I spent my three days off in bed. Bob was away. My mother was sure it was only my body telling me to slow down. I managed to fly for the next few weeks with great difficulty and kept mostly to myself.

* * *

There were weeks in a row when I felt invincible and believed I was truly beautiful. I would walk past store windows and look into the reflective glass thinking I ought to be Miss Singapore. I wanted to do lots and lots of things all at the same time. I spent endless hours at the library doing research for my diploma, always enthusiastic, never feeling tired or bored. I knew I was not getting enough sleep but I felt happy, healthy and energetic, which allowed me to give the very best in-flight service.

I was aware that I talked a lot, sometimes too much and usually too fast, not always to a receptive audience. I was often on an indescribable high with Bob. There were also times when I had screaming fits in the most unlikely situations when no one, not even I, could have seen such an over-reaction coming. Like the time when we were waiting for a car to pull out of a parking lot at the old Orchard Road carpark opposite Centrepoint. As Bob was about to reverse into the lot, a small car zipped in. I jumped out of our moving car, banged on the hood of the other car and asked him who the fuck he thought he was. I stood by his door and yelled at him to move out.

'You knew, you stupid prick! We had our indicator on. We were waiting for this spot. You knew!' I screamed. The driver just stared ahead through his windscreen and refused to budge. People walking within the carpark were looking at me. Bob parked in a way that would not block other cars and came to get me, taking my hand and walking me to the car. I was trembling.

'People cannot do things like that. They are thugs and bullies. And you let him get away with it,' I said, as I buckled my seat belt, still burning with rage. 'Please, let's just go home. Let's run these errands another day.'

'It's not about letting them get away with anything,' Bob said. 'There are people who behave badly but that does not mean you should stoop to their level. You just cannot behave like that, Mahita. It's most undignified and just not proper to lose control.' This was what Bob would say each time. And each time I would apologise and promise myself I would try harder to manage my temper the next time.

* * *

During these periods, I also believed I was absolutely amongst the few smartest stewardesses in Singapore Airlines. Everyone else was slow or not quite as clever. I was on top of the world and felt like an empress. Life was a magic carpet ride for me.

'If you don't mind me saying, Mahita, but I think you need to see a *sinseh*, a Chinese physician, to check your balance. I think your body is too hot,' said Peter, a steward who was positively gay. We had flown together several times and I knew he was not making a pass at me.

'What? I know what a *sinseh* is and there's no way I'm going to drink ginseng brewed with deer horn and sea horses and what-have-you to cool my body down. No way! What makes you say my body is too hot?' I asked, knowing what he meant and surprised that he would take the liberty to talk about something so personal.

'Don't get angry if I tell you okay, please, but the others think so too. They made me the spokesperson because they know you and I are close. All three of us are a bit worried. We think your energy level is not normal. Ling's parents are both *sinsehs* and she knows a lot about heaty and cooling things to eat to balance your body,' he said. 'She noticed you were eating a lot of red meat, chocolate and deep-fried foods, especially in Brussels. We haven't seen anyone eat so much chocolate or beef before. Those alone can make you like that,' said Peter. We were on the last leg of an eighteen-day trip around various cities in Europe and had spent a lot of time together shopping and sightseeing along with a few other crew members.

'Make me like what? Was I bothersome? Why did you not say something earlier, Peter? I know my body is heaty because of my diet but how can that make me more energetic? It's not like I'm bouncing off walls,' I said. 'Usually I just get angry, very angry. I don't remember losing my temper on this trip.'

'Wah! You really don't know yourself. It was like watching someone on a trampoline and yes, you did lose your temper. Remember that lady at the food court in Paris?' I did remember as Peter mentioned it – I had tried to forget it – but at that moment I wanted so badly to permanently delete it from my memory. It had happened over a week earlier, on that same flight. 'Yes, she was extremely rude but we were so glad we were not standing right next to you when you told her off. Really cannot! Cannot say such things to people even if it might be true.' Peter was referring to the Vietnamese lady serving at one of the counters. She ignored me a few times and by the time the third person behind me was served, I pointed out that it was my turn and she had already ignored me twice.

'Ya, okay! What you want?' she scowled, her eyes glaring.

'What do I want? I want you to learn some manners. I am also a waitress and I know you cannot treat your customers like this.' My voice was getting louder with every other word. I could feel people around me staring. I should have stopped talking then but I could not. The Vietnamese woman, who looked like she was in her mid to late twenties was also staring at me, with one hand holding a disposable plate. 'What I want is for you to get on a slow boat and head back to Vietnam. And just as you reach your shores, I hope your boat capsizes and that you get eaten by sharks! You bitch!' I turned around in an exaggerated huff and walked to where my colleagues were. One of them, Cecilia, was getting a drink not far from that counter and had seen and heard everything. No one said a word. It was likely that they did not understand what I said, not even the Vietnamese woman at whom

I was screaming. My tone and the expression on my face was, however, understood by everyone.

I lost my appetite so I sat and waited for the rest to finish their lunch, after which we did some sight-seeing. That night, I thought about my encounter with the Vietnamese woman and wondered about the source of such anger. Yet again I had tried but could not stop my cruel words from being spewed forth so quickly and loudly.

'Oh no! Cecilia must have told you. That was terrible, I agree. The server really was a bitch but I should not have said all that. Very undignified, as Bob would say. But what else about my behaviour makes you feel I need a *sinseh*?'

'Terrible? It was scary! We don't know French law. You could have been arrested for disorderly behaviour or verbal assault or, worse, racism. So lucky no one reported you.'

'I didn't think of that. I should have but I didn't. I guess I have to be more careful next time.' As I said this, I wondered how I was going to be more careful. I could never anticipate an outburst, let alone control the content and the volume. 'So, what else, Peter? I lost my temper. Big deal. It still does not warrant a visit to the *sinseh*.'

'Walking around the old city in Vienna, all of us needed a break except you. After the museum, hours before going to that budget opera, we needed a nap or wanted to relax in the room for a few hours, but you continued to explore the city. On top of that you were walking fast and talked so much, could not shut up even for a second,' Peter said all this without a hint of annoyance or malice in his voice. I could not believe what I was hearing even though I knew all of it to be true. 'Heatiness means a hot body. Too much *yang* means too much hot energy which makes you very energetic. Good for sex, I guess, but not really good overall. Quite unnerving for those around you,' he said. 'I'll take you there. Ling will meet us at her parents' medicine shop. Or we can go to another *sinseh* if you prefer.'

Initially I did not know what to make of Peter's frankness. I was taken aback and a bit hurt. I was also grateful that he wanted to help. On that flight, three crew members had noticed and agreed that my behaviour was odd. The last time my behaviour was referred to as odd or wrong, I was eighteen and Amah had spoken about *yin* and *yang*. I was now nearly twenty-four and I was having a similar discussion.

'Thanks for telling me, Peter. I appreciate the offer but I have a list of *yin* foods at home and will change my diet for a few weeks and see how it goes,' I said. I knew it was a temporary solution but wanted to start with remedies I already knew. I believed an imbalance was not as big a problem as some Chinese people thought it was. I was not going to give up meat and chocolate just to lower my energy levels. I decided if people could not cope with my high energy, I was happy to be left alone to enjoy the destinations to which I flew.

I had just moved in with Bob a month earlier, after my mother and sister emigrated to America. He had bought a small flat close to the airport with a sea view. While we were making dinner, I told him about the conversation with Peter. As I spoke, it occurred to me that the sheer length of that trip was enough to make anyone notice idiosyncrasies in other people's behaviour. While Bob had experienced various outbursts and chose to ignore or downplay them, I was shaken by the thought that living together could mean that he would notice things about me like Peter and the other crew members had.

'Did you tell the steward about what happened in Rome a few months ago?' Bob asked, remembering something I had clean forgotten until he mentioned it.

'You know, I had completely forgotten it. I try not to remember these things. They make me feel so bad about myself. This one, in particular, because it involved a child.'

* * *

It was at least six months earlier and I was walking along one of Rome's most famous streets, Via Veneto, where much of the 1960 movie *La Dolce Vita* was set. As I walked past Café de Paris, immortalised in the movie, I was surrounded by a small group of children no more than ten years old. I had been warned about these gypsy pickpockets and was very careful about keeping my handbag close to me. I was not prepared for their aggressiveness and tactics. There were several other tourists; the street was crowded and the pickpockets were quite well hidden amongst the crowds. The gypsy children ignored my pleas, which quickly turned to demands, to go away and started closing in on me while reaching for my pockets and bag. Incensed, I pushed the boy in front of me. He tripped, fell off the kerb and landed on his hands and bottom on the side of the street. He stared at me in disbelief. I was by now yelling at these gypsy children and was about to push another one but the gang broke up and ran, with the one on the street now out of sight. He was never in danger of being hit by a car but he could have been hurt had he hit his head when he fell. I felt a little violated by that whole experience so it was hard to feel any remorse at the time. However, I did feel bad later when I went back to my room that evening and thought about my day. I was glad there weren't any crew with me to witness what I had done. The few tourists who did see me push the pickpocket did not seem to care.

* * *

'I don't know anything about *yin* and *yang* so I can't comment but you have nothing to lose so just go and see a *sinseh*. Frankly, I don't think there's anything wrong with you. I think all you need is some self-control. You've always said your dad had a quick temper. You're no different. Learn self-control, that's all,' said Bob. It was a relief to hear him saying that. There was nothing wrong with me. Self-control at that moment sounded so easy.

* * *

This cycle of rage, magic and emptiness lasted all through my six years at Singapore Airlines. By now I had amassed an impressive collection of songs in my head that accompanied me through many days of extreme joy and sadness. One of my favourites for lifting my spirits was 'Don't Stop' by Fleetwood Mac, a song which urged me not to stop thinking about tomorrow, reminding me that yesterday was gone and that the next day was going to be better. I was convinced that some songs lied but I continued to listen to them anyway.

One evening, just before the end of those six years and while on a trip to Gold Coast in Australia, I called Bob in Singapore.

'I can't do this anymore. I am so tired and just so … I don't know. Empty. I feel empty,' I sobbed uncontrollably. 'It doesn't make sense, I had a splendid dinner with some lovely crew, my inflight supervisor is Michael Chong, one of the best inflight supervisors anyone could ask for, and all I want to do is rest my weary head on a pillow and never wake up. I can't be a stewardess for another day, Bob. I simply cannot do this anymore.'

'Then quit. I'll support you until you find a job. You need to serve your notice so you'll still have to somehow make it for another month.' That was his very kind and encouraging response. 'Quit,' he said, just like that,.

The morning after I returned from that flight, in early July, I went into the Cabin Crew Office and handed in my resignation. On the eighth day of the eight month of the eighty-eighth year – 8/8/88, a most auspicious day for the Chinese, eight being associated with wealth – my life as a stewardess with the world's number one airline came to a screeching halt.

Although I'd had my ups and downs, grown as a person, made some amazing friends, broadened my horizons with constant travelling and earned a diploma, I soon realised that for six years I had been nothing but a waitress in the sky.

CHAPTER 3

'I have love in me the likes of which you can scarcely imagine
and rage the likes of which you would not believe. If I cannot
satisfy the one, I will indulge the other.'

Mary Shelley

So what now? I was nearly twenty-six years old, without a
college degree and had just spent six years of my life as a glorified
waitress. Other than a diploma for kindergarten teaching which I
tried and found to be quite dull, I was not qualified for much else.
I was not interested in being a guest relations officer in a hotel,
which was what many stewardesses did when they quit flying.
The pretty face in the red cheongsam, that elegant Chinese Suzie
Wong-style dress with the mandarin collar and slits up to there
and working the graveyard shift was just not my thing. Nor did I
want to be a sales assistant or a receptionist, both of which seemed
like typical options. Most Singaporeans I knew had a rather low
opinion of stewardesses, assuming all of us to be brainless party
girls. This was quite unfair and unjustified, but their perceptions
were also their reality and I had to either try, at least, to change

those perceptions or be interviewed by someone with a more open mind.

How was I going to convince a prospective employee I was more than just a dolled-up face with a bright smile? That I had the smarts to apply anything I learnt?

* * *

I started my life as a newly resigned stewardess by sleeping a lot. There were days when I was glued to my bed and was overly sensitive to light. Bob and I blamed it on years of insufficient sleep finally catching up. We saw this need for sleep as being good and natural. I was also consumed by worry and emptiness. I had very little appetite even for my favourite foods. What Bob did not know was that after more than six years, three of which were spent living together, I was aching for a marriage proposal. His reluctance was baffling. He knew my green card application for emigration to America was being processed and that I did not want to get married before my green card was issued. He also knew that I would only emigrate if things did not work between us. I decided to be patient. I had no family in Singapore and my patience had turned to fear for my future, the comfortable one as a pilot's wife I had dreamed of. My confidence and self-esteem had plummeted to a new low.

On days like this, a song played in my head, 'The Sound of

Silence'. I would start by saying 'Hello, darkness,' and talk to it like an old friend.

It took about ten days before I snapped out of my listlessness. I dived straight into looking for a job.

* * *

After hearing that kindergarten teachers were paid about four hundred dollars a month, I decided to consider something else. Without any idea what I wanted to do, I sent out job applications for positions I found in the classifieds ranging from trainee or junior buyer to administration executive to bank teller. Most jobs stipulated they wanted only Chinese applicants. This was long before Singapore banned such advertisements. With a limited number of positions available for non-Chinese, I sent out about thirty applications. I did not get even one interview. Those who responded said I did not have the right experience or did not speak Mandarin. When I called and asked about training for junior or trainee positions, where experience was not required, I received a mumbled response about calling me back. No one did. I wondered if I would ever get a job.

I decided to reconsider working in a kindergarten and eventually found a position as a teacher's aide at Singapore Preparatory School, a small international school catering to students from three to eight years old. I assisted a teacher in a class of three-year-olds. My salary was two hundred and fifty dollars. I took it for the experience, hoping I would find something better after a few months. Although I liked the hours, the job was boring; as an aide, I could only carry out the teacher's instructions. I was not allowed to initiate any activity. I felt I was being dumbed down from the lack of stimulation. I quit after a month.

Meanwhile, I spent my time reading and catching up with my friends. Bob was flying on regional routes so he was often home. I liked spending my time with him and with my friends, not working for a change. I knew I would soon get bored.

About two months after my stint at the kindergarten, and just before Christmas, Bob and I had an argument.

'I am tired of waiting, Bob. I am tired of my mother's friends asking when I'm getting married. I hate it when I can just hear that voice in their heads saying that Indian girls from good families would be disowned for such a sinful relationship. You have no idea what it's like,' I ranted on. He mumbled something again and I thought I heard the question I had been waiting to hear for the longest time.

'What did you say?' I asked, cautious about not getting my hopes too high.

'Let's get married then,' he said.

'Really?' That was all I could think of to say, followed seconds later, when his words sank in, with an enthusiastic 'Yes! Oh Bob, yes!'

With that, the argument ended and we were engaged. Even though I felt cheated of a traditional or romantic proposal, I was overjoyed. There was no ring because he had not planned to propose, not just yet anyway. He promised we would go shopping for one soon, and we did. In the early months after the engagement, with the pretty diamond ring on my finger, I was in a state of perpetual bliss. My body and mind synchronised – I felt a certain calm and peacefulness, a state of security I had never felt before.

I was very, very happy for months.

At the start of the New Year, I was offered a position at a family friend's small trading company. It was a good introduction to working in an office and using a computer. I learnt a little about logistics and trading in electronics but the job itself was not challenging. I thought I would stick it out until I had enough experience to try something else. It also kept me focused so that the stress of planning a wedding was slightly reduced when it became a distraction.

In the weeks leading up to the wedding, I felt my mind was racing out of control. I slept late and woke up early; I needed very little sleep. Although I was easily distracted and agitated, I thought I was coping well with the stress of planning a major life event without the help of Bob's family or mine, all of whom lived abroad. I ended up throwing two major tantrums. Bob was present both times and though used to my occasional outbursts he was stunned into silence by both the ferocity and suddenness of my reaction in these two instances. I remember the instances so vividly because both times I went to bed asking myself if I was becoming cuckoo. Before that, I never wondered about my outbursts and like everyone around me, including Bob, I just accepted that I had a bad temper and was unpredictable.

The first incident was at the catering manager's office at the hotel where we planned to hold the wedding banquet. It was a few nights before the wedding and we were finalising the menu and seating arrangements. All our Western guests and only a fraction of my Asian friends had responded. I had no time to follow up with phone calls and could not make any assumptions about their attendance. I suddenly stood up and started screaming.

'Fuck them! This is the perfect definition of good manners, Asian style. Maybe I'm supposed to assume they're all coming simply because they would not miss something so important to me. Why can't they just say so? Because they're too fucking important to call, that's fucking why!' I said. 'Oh I know what! If they turn up, let's have them sit outside. The carpark, yes, sitting on the floor and we'll serve them dinner on banana leaves. They'll eat with their hands. We'll give them finger bowls. What fun! It's the least we can do for such rude and thoughtless people.' Without warning, I grabbed the pieces of paper on which the guests' names and table numbers had been typed out and tore the pages up before throwing them in the air and storming out of the catering manager's office. I walked quickly towards the car, sobbing, and waited for Bob to catch up.

I had calmed down by the time Bob reached the car. He was his usual calm self and before I could apologise for what seemed felt like madness to me at the time, he took a deep breath and I knew he was going to say something upsetting. I also knew I deserved whatever was coming my way.

'Are you sure you want to go through with this? Maybe you're not ready,' he said gently, looking at me.

I was too ashamed to look at him. We were still in the car and had not left the carpark. I stared out the windscreen towards the hotel lobby, wondering if this was when Bob would talk about breaking up.

'No, no, Bob, please don't say that.' I was terrified at the prospect of losing Bob, knowing I could only blame myself. 'Of course I am ready. I've been ready since I met you. Let's get married. Please. Things will get better, I promise. It is just so stressful. I am so sorry,' I begged.

'You simply cannot behave like this. You only embarrass yourself. And for goodness sake, please stop using the F word. It is so undignified. You look and sound repulsive when you get yourself into such a state,' he said. 'Stress management is what you need. Go and buy some books and start some serious reading.'

'Yes, Bob that would be a good idea. I haven't been able to master self-control on my own. It's not like I don't try. I really cannot feel it coming. And when it does, I just cannot stop. I'll practice what the books preach and that should work,' I said.

'What do you mean you can't see it coming? Sure you can! We all can. Again, it boils down to self-control. Maybe you're just ignoring the signs,' he said. 'Get some books and take it from there.'

Ignoring the signs. I had never thought about that. I never saw any signs but I made a mental note to look for some relevant books after the wedding. I always thought only inadequate people read self-help books, but I so badly wanted to be Bob's perfect wife that I decided I could probably handle one or two books on anger management. I hoped to understand what made me a destructive raving lunatic in minutes, without warning, after I realised my behaviour could have led to the catering manager calling for Security to throw me out of the hotel premises. I was glad she did not. I was so caught up with the wedding preparations that I did not bother to get the books.

The second incident took place a week later, the night before the wedding. I was sleeping over, together with my mother and aunt, at my friend Vidula's home. She was going to be my maid of honour at the wedding. All afternoon and right through dinner I was highly excitable and restless. My favourite aunt, Aunty Pushpa, gave me a Valium tablet and insisted I had an early night. She wanted me to be well-rested for my big day. By ten thirty that night, I was fast asleep.

Several hours later, my mother roused me from a deep sleep and said there was a call for me. Groggy and disoriented from the Valium, I walked slowly to the living room.

'Hi, it's me. I just flew in for your wedding.' The voice on the other end was soft and gentle. It was my friend Vishal. 'Hello? Are you there?'

'Hi,' I said after a long pause. My head was spinning. I looked at the clock. It was about two in the morning. My head hurt and I needed to get back to sleep.

'It's 2 a.m. I'm getting married tomorrow. I was fast asleep and so was the entire household until the phone rang. How the hell did you know I was here?' I asked.

'I called your house and Bob gave me your number. He did say to call you tomorrow,' he replied. 'But I just got back and couldn't wait to tell you that I've flown all the way from Rochester, New York, just to be at your wedding.'

'I don't remember inviting you. I didn't even think about it because I thought you'd be away. Why would you fly all the way down for my wedding?' I was starting to feel more awake now although still more groggy than awake.

'I was planning to come back for a short summer break anyway but I thought I'd come a week earlier so I could be at the wedding and stay for a few weeks. So what are the details? Where, when?'

'I can't think straight. I'll call you tomorrow,' I said and hung up.

I went back to bed but could not get back to sleep. Soon, I was wide awake and trembling from anger. I no longer thought of Vishal as my friend but a most inconsiderate person whose self-importance was so misplaced he could not think of my need for sleep before the most important day of my life. I did not want to see him and decided I would call him in the morning to ask him not to come to the wedding. After tossing and turning for about three hours, I fell asleep.

I woke up the next morning feeling like I had a nasty hangover. Aunty Pushpa said it was the broken sleep under the effects of Valium. I had forgotten about the call until she reminded me. I picked up the phone to call Vishal. As I dialled the number, I felt ill. I hung up and called Bob instead.

'Vishal called me at two this morning and I was so angry I couldn't get back to sleep until nearly five. I am so tired, Bob. I feel hungover,' I said.

'I told him specifically not to call you until this morning. I'm sorry, I shouldn't have given him the number. I would have expected him to know better,' said Bob.

'He's too fucking thoughtless to know better, Bob! He did not care that he was robbing me of much-needed sleep fifteen hours before my wedding. He even woke you up! He's an idiot, Bob! A thoughtless, fucking idiot and I don't want him there!' I was hysterical and suddenly became aware of the silence in the living room of my maid of honour's house. 'Please Bob, please call him and tell him I do not want to see him. He must not be at the wedding,' I said, by now in tears.

'Are you sure? He's already here and yes, what he did was stupid and thoughtless but he has flown all the way from the U.S. just to see you get married. Do you want me to ask him just to come to the wedding and not the dinner? I'll explain that the seating arrangements have been finalised and it's too late to make changes,' Bob said in his typical gracious tone and manner.

'No! No, Bob! I do not want to see him. I never invited him. I do not want to see a selfish fuck who calls me at two in the morning just before my wedding. I did not get enough sleep and now I will be a wreck all day. Tell him you'll kill him if you see him anywhere near the church. Tell him! I'll kill him myself! Tell him, Bob! You must!' I was screaming and swearing like a lowlife and was an emotional mess. Everyone around me was quiet, waiting for me to end the call. My mother later told me it was the foul language that bothered them more than the screaming.

'Okay. As you wish. I'll call him and ask him not to come to the wedding,' Bob said in a soft, kind voice. I thanked him and told him I would see him soon.

Several months after this incident, when Vishal returned for Christmas break, he called and asked what happened that day. I told him how I had felt and what I had said to Bob.

'You really said all those things about me?' The incredulity in his tone was unmistakable.

'Yes. I was very angry and upset. You were thoughtless. I'm not going to apologise, if that's why you are calling,' I said.

'No, I'm not asking for an apology. Just wanted to know what happened.'

'Now you know,' I said and, feeling forgiving, invited him out for lunch. 'Let's go for chicken rice at Swee Kee. Noon tomorrow?'

'Tomorrow's good. I have an appointment near Middle Road. I can be there by noon.'

Since that day, Vishal has become one of my closest and most loyal friends. Before he got married and left Singapore, he saw in me those same rages that I displayed during my Singapore Airlines days. Like all my close friends, he never judged me or abandoned me and just believed I was extremely mercurial and had a violent temper. None of my friends thought something could be wrong with me.

* * *

My mother, Aunty Pushpa and Vidula were very concerned but blamed it on that noxious cocktail of wedding jitters, insufficient sleep and the residual effects of Valium. They insisted I have some breakfast and maybe try to sleep for another hour or two. It was not even ten in the morning and I did not have to leave the house until about four that afternoon.

Lying in bed that morning in Vidula's room, I replayed in my muddled head the two scenes of the past week and the monster into which I had rapidly morphed. I pictured Bob's soft, kind face and imagined his gentle voice. I thought about all the good things that defined him. He possessed in plenitude all the qualities of a true gentleman and perfect husband – intelligent, funny, honest, highly principled, fiercely loyal, patient, generous and most important, consistent in all of the above. He also had impeccable manners, a stable job, was a filial son and, up until we were engaged, a very eligible bachelor surrounded by young, eager stewardesses ready to take my place.

I thought about his worst qualities and could think of just one – his wretched critical eye which was inextricably linked to his mouth. If I put on a little too much weight in the wrong place – on my small forty-two-kilogram frame – he would not only notice it, he would also tell me about it. It would never occur to him that some criticisms were hurtful regardless of the softness of the delivery. With the emphasis I placed on all that was good about him, I honestly believed that just one bad quality was more than compensated for by all his good qualities.

I felt blessed. He was everything I could wish for in a husband. He had so much to offer. I wondered what I had to offer him in return. I could see why he took so long to propose. He was uncertain about what kind of wife I would be. He had seen me at my best and my worst. Still, he had his pick and yet he chose me.

At that moment, with the wedding hours away, I could not see why he still wanted to marry me. He deserved better. I believed I deserved less.

I tried to get some sleep, but sleep eluded me. Soon after, I gave up trying, had a late lunch and started the long process of dressing up as a bride with Vidula next to me doing the same, getting ready to be my maid of honour. When I looked in the mirror, I felt beautiful, joyous and ready to walk down the aisle to take my vows in front of God and a hundred other people.

In the summer of 1989, less than a year after I quit Singapore Airlines, I married Bob, just as I had said I would nearly seven years before. We were married at Orchard Road Presbyterian Church, one of the oldest churches in Singapore. On the arms of my uncle who had flown in from Toronto with his family, I walked down the aisle in my ivory gown made from Thai silk, Belgian lace and faux pearls. I thought what a stellar job my friend Emily had done with the flowers on the pews. As I got closer to end of the aisle, I saw Bob in a black tuxedo and thought he looked more handsome and nervous than I had ever seen him before.

The ceremony was over in an hour and everyone headed to the Marco Polo hotel at the other end of Orchard Road for a cocktail and dinner reception. For our wedding song, I chose 'Follow You, Follow Me' by Genesis. I liked it for its simplicity and sentiment. I meant it when I told Bob through the song that I felt secure with him, no longer fearful and that I am better for what he gives to me. I told him through the same song that while I lived I would follow him and stay with him through all the days and nights. Those few hours from the moment I started to get ready for the wedding until that dance were the happiest hours of my life. I did not know what absolute joy and peace felt like until then. I wanted the feeling to last forever.

Soon after I got married, I had decided that working in a small local family firm just wasn't stimulating enough but I had no idea what I was going to do next and where to begin looking for a job in an international firm. While talking to my friend Neeta one evening, she suggested a career in advertising. She was then working at The Ball Partnership which, in the early Nineties, was the hottest advertising agency in town. She encouraged me to apply to the top twenty agencies, kindly offering to get me a list of addresses with contact details and saying that it was an industry desperate for talent. For some reason, agencies could not attract fresh graduates and were willing to consider people like me, without qualifications but who could be trained. I thought I would give it a shot. I had nothing to lose.

I was very keen to work with Ogilvy & Mather, having been inspired by David Ogilvy's book, *Confessions of an Advertising Man*, which I had read several years before. I loved his memoir about how he dropped out of Oxford University and went on to do odd jobs, including being a chef in Paris and selling ovens in Scotland, to becoming the granddaddy of advertising. After six years with the world's number one airline, I wanted to be with the world's number one advertising agency.

So badly did I want a job at Ogilvy & Mather that I presented them with a win-win situation – confident I was cut out for advertising, I offered to work for free for three months. I never heard back from them. Two follow-up calls went unreturned. I was extremely disappointed and assumed that the top agency would never consider a candidate lacking in educational qualifications. I had to try my luck elsewhere. Armed with Neeta's list of the top twenty agencies along with the names of their managing directors, I set out to create an application letter that would guarantee a response. As every managing director had a western name, I took the liberty of being a bit more brave with my application. It was simple, honest, and with Bob's help and touch of wit, it was also clever and funny. I used direct marketing which included a leaflet listing a few skills and ideal personality traits for the position along with a check box and a self-addressed stamped envelope and wrote to just the top twelve agencies. All except Ogilvy & Mather responded with interest within a week. It was overwhelming. Even Neeta believed it must have been the quality of the application.

Bob bought me my first expensive suit and I interviewed at four agencies in two days and had other interviews lined up over the next week. I could not believe how easy it was. Neeta said that as someone just starting out, I should base my decision on the client list and not the agency ranking. After all, I had only applied to agencies in which I was interested.

The first offer came from D'Arcy Masius Benton & Bowles (DMB&B) with my key account being Procter & Gamble. At 7:30 p.m. on a Thursday night in the managing director's office, I said yes, absolutely yes, and gushed my thanks. I signed my contract the next day and started work on the Monday morning four days later.

In January 1990, I started a new life in advertising. A life perfectly suited to the mentally ill in an industry where psychosis thrives, as I would find out over the next fifteen years.

CHAPTER 4

'Advertising is the most fun you can have
with your clothes on.'
Bill Cosby

I loved the advertising business from the moment I sat at
my imposing dark brown desk and faced thick heavy files of
documents placed there for my 'reading pleasure'. I don't think
anyone realised that it really was my pleasure. There was so much
to learn and I could not wait. By the end of my first week, I felt
as if I had leap-frogged into graduate school. I remembered Mark
Twain's words: 'All you need is ignorance and confidence and the
success is sure.'

Certainly I was ignorant and I was confident. I was also very,
very hungry. I wanted to learn. I was not overly ambitious, I did
not think about how far I could go in a number of years. All I
wanted was to be as good as I could possibly be. I found myself in
the right place at the right time.

My boss, Chris Ang, stood out for being clever, funny and
full of insights. He headed the Procter & Gamble account in

Asia Pacific and was very likeable. Everything I learnt about the industry, the fundamentals of marketing, and the discipline required in a well-written strategic brief or client proposal, I learnt from Chris. The most important lesson he taught me, one that I would apply in every role in every office, was to challenge the client if I felt they were wrong or if I could offer other solutions. Growing up in a country where it was not common practice to challenge people or ideas, I was not sure if it was good advice at first. It was only after several meetings at the client's office when I saw that Chris was right. It soon became obvious to me that most clients enjoyed a client-is-king relationship with their agency and did not take too kindly to being questioned. Only a few clients, invariably smart and confident, could see the merit in engaging in a discussion. I was in my element with such clients.

DMB&B was probably the twelfth agency on my priority list and certainly did not have a high profile. It was a big agency in America, headquartered in New York, and before the days of multiple mergers and acquisitions, the agency was well-known for creating some enduring icons like Budweiser's 'This Bud's for you' and Coca-Cola's Santa Claus, which paved the way for Santa as we know him today – overweight and jolly with a white beard, dressed in a red suit, black boots and thick wide belt. In DMB&B's relatively small agency in Singapore, we told these stories with pride. It was an aggressive little agency out for more business which it needed to survive. This meant constant pitching which I thoroughly enjoyed. My real work for clients had to wait until the end of the day, which in turn meant working late into the night. I had the energy and drive so I did not mind locking up the office between nine and eleven o'clock nearly every night.

Working with the very bright and genuinely nice people at Procter & Gamble, I soon realised that I loved to be engaged in intellectually stimulating discussions on strategies and creative concepts. I handled Whisper feminine hygiene, known as Always in most countries outside Asia. It took some getting used to in the beginning, when discussing strategies, to focus on the fact that we were ultimately selling women a cleaner, drier feeling and more security *down there*.

Chris was also a mentor and often reminded me that it was a privilege to work with the world's pre-eminent consumer goods company. Procter & Gamble was one of several accounts I juggled with Burger King, one of the agency's biggest clients in terms of billings, and Philips Domestic Appliances. As the workload on other accounts got heavier, I was taken off Procter & Gamble.

Eight months after joining DMB&B, I thought it was time to start thinking about motherhood. I was twenty-eight and Bob was thirty-eight. With his flying schedules and my long hours and weekends at the office, we knew it could take a while, so planning ahead was necessary. We took all the blood tests required. We decided we would start trying during a holiday to Europe, which was six months away.

Somewhere around late March 1991 while we were on holiday, I conceived. It took six months before we learnt I was having twins. It was a most difficult pregnancy; I was hospitalised twice, the first time for a threatened miscarriage and the second for being so sick that I lost half a kilo a day over four days. Each time, Bob was fortunate enough to be able to be taken off his long flights and placed on standby for short regional trips. He was very caring and mindful of my physical condition, ensuring I ate nutritious meals at regular intervals. When my cravings kicked in around the third month – beer, of all things – he bought every brand of non-alcoholic beer for me to try until I found the one I liked best. This was quite a challenge as I was never keen on beer so during my pregnancy I could not know what I liked or did not like until I tried it. We eventually settled on a German brew, the only non-alcoholic beer I thought tasted like the real thing. Years later, Bob would joke about how the kids drove me to drink even before they were born.

I worked from my hospital bed, writing creative briefs and catching up on correspondence with clients and colleagues. Colleagues brought work to me at my insistence because they knew I needed to keep my mind working. My brain thrived on writing and thinking; although I read a lot of fiction during that time, I missed what I did at work. In between hospital stays, I went back to work for about six hours a day. My colleagues, bosses and most clients were extremely supportive and actively yanked work from under me just so I could keep shorter hours. I never forgot their kindness. Difficult pregnancy notwithstanding, I felt very energetic, my mind constantly racing with concurrent thoughts of work, impending motherhood, and house-hunting. We needed a bigger home to accommodate two babies and a live-in helper.

At eighteen weeks, just days before my first scheduled scan, I contracted chicken pox. Having a childhood illness during adulthood is hard enough, the symptoms being more severe, the itchiness and blistering unrelenting. Having chicken pox during a stressful pregnancy made me desperate. Never a religious person, I started reading the Bible. As a Hindu-raised, Catholic-school-educated agnostic, I was not expecting to be comforted but the poetic verses of the King James Bible did comfort me while making the Bible a good and interesting read.

On the basis that twins are often early, I went on unpaid leave about six weeks before my due date. Two weeks later, we moved in to our new flat and two days after that, my twin daughters, Elena and Caroline, were born. Although they were nearly a month early, jaundiced and tiny, I was relieved that eight months of pregnancy had come to an end. Motherhood had just begun and when I held them for the first time, I was not sure if I was ready to be a mother.

Bob was a most devoted and attentive husband throughout my pregnancy. That devotion and attention was extended to the babies the moment they arrived. We had a competent live-in helper who had two sets of twins a year apart, which made it easier for me to trust my babies to her care and return to work after two months. When the babies were two weeks old and I was still on maternity leave, I went in to the office every Friday morning to catch up on correspondence and work in progress. Despite my body having been traumatised by naturally delivering two babies, I felt in fine form. In the early months of their birth, despite waking up every few hours for their feeds, I often felt energised during the day. My mind needed the stimulation that only work could offer. I also missed my friends at work.

A few months before the babies' first birthday, I started to change. I started to feel tired and weepy. I slept in and took naps every weekend and drank up to four cans of Diet Coke a day and still felt the same. There was a familiarity to what I was feeling; I had been through this 'phase' before, but it felt like rather a long time ago and under very different circumstances. I put it down to exhaustion brought on by too many weeks in a row of ruthlessly long hours at work while still learning to cope with twins. I was also fed up with the helper who turned out to be rude, arrogant and lazy. I fired her and although I felt better when the new helper arrived, I still did not feel completely well. I saw a family doctor who referred me to a psychiatrist, Dr Lee, whose clinic was just one floor up from our family doctor's office. Both were housed in an old building just up the road from my home.

'I think you might have postpartum depression. Mood swings are normal with this condition. Or it could just be the stress. It cannot be easy having two babies, a husband who is away a lot and you working long hours,' said Dr Lee after asking me several questions. I told him about the times when I experienced emptiness for days on end and being told I have too much hot energy in my body. I wondered if all these feelings were related.

'I was fine from the time they were born. Is it possible there is something else? What about heatiness and my past experiences feeling numb and hollow? I am thirty years old and I cannot keep going on like this. I am so afraid I will do something bad to myself or my babies. Please tell me what to do, doctor. Please give me a pill or something,' I said, desperate to be rid of whatever was plaguing me.

'I believe in the balance of *yin* and *yang*, but what you have sounds more like postpartum depression. Try and make lifestyle changes first. I don't think you need medication just yet,' he said.

'A pill, Dr Lee, please. Put me on something that will make me a good mother who can cope with twins,' I said, almost begging. I do not know where I got the idea about the pill. Probably from watching too many American movies or television shows featuring characters who pop pills to make their problems go away or to cope better with day-to-day living.

'Try not to rely on medication. For now, maybe you can think of some ways to help yourself, which in turn will help your family life. You can start by cutting down your work hours. It seems to dominate your life and I wonder if it might be personal choice,' the doctor said in a tone I did not like.

'What do you mean by personal choice? Why would I choose to work long hours?' I shot back, not thrilled about being accused of choosing to spend more time at work. Deep down, I knew there was some truth to what he said.

'I have seen some parents who find the demands of raising a family so stressful that they deliberately stay back at work so they end up with less time for their children. They are usually parents like you who do not have the support of an extended family and rely entirely on a foreign helper. This is not uncommon, so do think about cutting back on your hours if it is possible,' he said. 'On weekends when you are all alone and cannot cope, leave the babies in their cots and just step outside your apartment for some time. Five minutes, half an hour. As long as you need. Sit by the door so you are close enough for their safety but removed enough to have time out,' he suggested.

'I've never thought of that. Sometimes I would think about leaving them in their rooms and running away. But there was never anywhere to go, so I stayed. By night time I would be cursing myself for such selfish thoughts. I'll do as you suggest,' I said.

'Find something pleasurable to do every evening as a routine. Exercise is very good for you, but even passive activities like reading or listening to music will help you relax after a stressful day,' he said. 'Try these for a while, establish a routine and see how it goes. If there is no improvement, we can discuss other options like medication and therapy. The next time you go through this, please see me or any doctor right away. For now, I don't think you have anything to worry about.'

Yet again, I was relieved there was nothing wrong with me. I immediately put into practice what the doctor suggested and after two weeks I felt a noticeable difference. I did not believe I had postpartum depression and was relieved to be back to my old self within a few weeks. I did not see the doctor again.

Just before Christmas, I received a box of Christmas and birthday presents from Sue. The birthday presents for the girls were opened and the Christmas presents went under the tree. Seeing the cutest little swimsuits and pool robes – such thoughtful gifts – a sense of happiness and gratitude for our friendship filled me. At that point, I missed Sue more than I had in the last few years. I wanted to tell her how I was feeling and asked her how she coped without help with her first child, born six months after the girls. Long-distance calls were too expensive for confiding problems and every time I started to write I thought of the urgency being lost in transit. Although I called Sue a couple of times a year, I kept the calls light-hearted. She was the only person I loved and trusted enough to talk to about my darkest fears yet I chose not to in the name of frugality – overseas calls were very expensive then – and convenience. I wanted so badly to ask her if she ever felt like leaving her baby sleeping in his crib, going for a long walk, getting lost and not wanting to be found. Did she ever think about going to the top of a tall building and jumping off it? Did it ever cross her mind how easy it would be to stop her baby from crying by putting a pillow over his face? And if she ever thought any or all of these things, what did she do? I never asked her any of these questions. I wanted her to hear only the good stuff from me, just as I was hearing from her.

Sometimes on Monday mornings after a stressful weekend of mothering, I hinted at my desperation to some colleagues but my tone was always flippant so I do not think anyone really took me seriously. I did everything I could to cope and was thankful that I did not hurt my babies during those dark moments.

When the girls were nearly two years old, things started to go rapidly downhill. The Burger King client's requirements for a series of television commercials and a new brand campaign meant shooting on Sundays and post production late at night or on weekends. I hardly saw my babies and when I did, it was brief, like stolen moments, and I was too drained to enjoy them.

After four years of long hours and weekends, trying to raise twin babies at the same time, I woke up one day and found myself delirious for no apparent reason. I went to work with great difficulty, calling a taxi instead of waiting as usual for the bus. I said hello to the usual people on my usual walk from the entrance to my desk. As soon as I sat down I started to sob, slowly, quietly at first and then I walked very quickly out the back door, down the fire exit and just cried and cried and cried.

Celeste, Chris' secretary, saw me as I was on my way out, said hello and sensing something was wrong, went back to her desk, told her boss she was going downstairs for a while and came looking for me. Sweet, lovely Celeste just put her arms around me and asked what she could do to help. She did not ask why.

'I am so tired, Celeste. I am just very, very tired. Sometimes I go to sleep thinking how nice it would be not to have to wake up in the morning or not to have to wake up at all. Oh Celeste, the babies deserve a better mother. Bob deserves a better wife,' I said between sobs.

'Don't say such things, Mahita! You are a good mother, wife, colleague and friend. I think you work too hard, that's all. Maybe you also take work too seriously and you let it get to you. It's just work. Your family is everything,' said Celeste as she handed me more tissues.

'You're right, Celeste. I'm losing the plot. Once I put my priorities in perspective, and spend more time on relaxation, I'll be fine. There is nothing wrong with me,' I said, feeling calmer with Celeste's arms around my shoulder.

'There is nothing wrong with you. I'm always here for you. You stay here. I'll get your things and tell whoever needs to know that you had to go home. Don't worry,' said Celeste as she leaned towards me and gave me a hug. We had worked closely together long enough for her to know I needed time out.

On that day, I took my first sick day in nearly four years, not counting the maternity sick days when I was pregnant and when the babies were born. I did not want to see the girls and could not eat. Bob was away. I wept while I shivered under the fan, at times comforted by the constant whirr of the dust-covered blades. I was terrified of these feelings, which I could not understand. They were much more intense than anything I had experienced before. I was confined to my bed for three days, unable to even leave my home to see a doctor. I was fortunate that Chris practised an honour system where staff did not always have to produce a medical certificate after taking sick days.

By the end of the third day, I was convinced that what I had was no cause for concern and was merely brought on by extreme stress due to working absurd hours. I decided I needed time off. A week later, I quit DMB&B.

* * *

After a month of staying at home and playing catch-up mothering with my children, I became restless and started looking for a job. It was the early Nineties and the Singapore economy was on an upswing. The advertising industry was still buoyant and though still competitive, jobs were available. I could not believe my luck when a chance encounter with a former client at Procter &

Gamble, who was by then Marketing Manager at McDonald's, led me to interview for a position at Leo Burnett as Account Manager.

Without much effort, I got the job. I loved being at Leo Burnett, working in an agency founded by one of the advertising industry's greatest and most famous people of all time. For me, Leo Burnett was on a pedestal with David Ogilvy.

This was shortly after Leo Burnett's Singapore office had been on a major cost-cutting exercise. With Singapore's astronomical rents in the central business district, Leo Burnett was forced to move a little too far away from every desirable area, eventually ending up in a dingy building in the less attractive side of Singapore's Little India. It was not in keeping with the image of an international advertising agency but with a limited rental budget, there was no other option. The area was certainly colourful and vibrant. It was not uncommon to have a transvestite prostitute – most likely an illegal worker from India – make a pass at an attractive male colleague while we sat as a group waiting for our fried rice at a corner coffee shop on Desker Road.

I missed some of my former colleagues, especially Celeste. However, it was motivating to work with the McDonald's team at Leo Burnett. I enjoyed the privilege of being part of the team able to convert legions of Singaporeans raised on divine street food and superb flavours of ethnic cuisine to switch to stodgy, bland pieces of meat stuffed between two slices of bread. With laksa, satay and chicken rice available on every corner, why would anyone choose the appropriately named junk food? It was clearly a brilliant marketing strategy crafted by McDonald's and Leo Burnett specifically for Singaporeans. As a true champion of Singapore food, I personally found this culinary degeneration a national tragedy. Our street food is amongst the most delicious and varied in the world – ten years later Anthony Bourdain would become a great fan and repeat visitor – so I should have been outraged. But I wasn't. After all, I was selling an experience first and foremost as promised in the tagline 'Good Times, Great Taste'. I was happy and felt my brain was finally getting the nourishment it had been craving for some time.

The best and most unforgettable part about my time managing the McDonald's account would have to be when I had to drive Ronald McDonald around one weekend for his visits to selected restaurants because the young lady whose job it was to do the driving was sick. As my helper was off on Sundays, I had no choice but to take my three-year-old twins along. They were thrilled when I told them they were going to meet Ronald McDonald. They had heard about him in kindergarten and seen him on television commercials. It was three in the afternoon, time for their one-hour nap but instead I had to get them ready to go out. They were very cooperative despite being tired. I drove to the McDonald's office which was just fifteen minutes up the road from my home. By the time I drove into the carpark the kids were fast asleep. As I parked, I saw Ronald McDonald stepping into the carpark. I woke the kids up gently and told them they had to walk to the van. They did as they were told, walking slowly and a little unsteadily like drunken little people and got in. Elena appeared nervous and obediently sat next to Ronald McDonald. Caroline wailed as soon as she got in and saw Ronald McDonald's face. She could not be consoled and as I was already running late, I had to beg her to stay with Elena and Ronald McDonald and assured her she had nothing to be afraid of. Ronald McDonald explained that kids reacted like this quite often, going from excited to terrified in seconds. For very young children, he said, images on a van and television are very different from seeing a live six-foot clown with the full make-up and bulbous red nose. I told Caroline I would be right in front driving them all. Ronald McDonald had a sweet red-bean bun in his pocket, which he split in two and gave one piece to each child. Elena took it, thanked him and ate it slowly. Caroline took it and held it in her small hand while she continued crying. Within minutes, her crying wound down to a soft, laboured sob. Ronald gently picked her up and she let him place her on his lap. Within minutes she had fallen asleep in his arms. I turned to look at them at the traffic stop. It was the sweetest sight.

The next day, the girls told their friends in kindergarten about meeting Ronald McDonald. No one seemed to believe them. They were only three years old and had just started kindergarten a few months earlier. Soon after, I had a few mothers calling me, asking how they could go about arranging a ride in the van with Ronald McDonald. I explained it was for work and only for that weekend. My children felt quite privileged that whole week, just from the two hours with Ronald McDonald. I felt so proud for making that happen. It was spontaneous, out of necessity and did not cost a cent. I gave myself a small star for that.

* * *

Mania served me well at Leo Burnett. I needed the energy for those never-ending days and weekends. I enjoyed a good relationship with my clients, especially Fanny and Kenneth. Just as I was drawn to their sharp minds, I think they were drawn to my enthusiasm and passion for their business. However, after several months, my mania started to show its ugly side. The rages came back. I was working closely with a client who was inclined towards the client-is-king approach in the client-agency relationship. While generally sweet-natured and totally harmless, she was like many clients I had worked with at DMB&B; she rarely *asked* for anything, she *told* me what she wanted; she hardly ever suggested changes to creative concepts, she gave instructions and insisted the changes be made.

One day, after a phone discussion about some changes on a tray liner for yet another promotion, I walked in a huff from my room to the creative department. On the way, I saw my boss, the account director, who asked for an update. Screaming, I called the client an idiot and ranted about the insignificant changes which did nothing to enhance the tray liner. It did not cross my mind that it was not even worth getting worked up over something so small but I simply could not rein myself in. My voice echoed through the stairwell and when my boss asked me to do as the client asked, I banged my fist against a wall. It was a thick plaster wall with a rough paint finish. I hurt myself, but not enough to notice in my deranged state. My boss was startled but did not know how to react other than to look at me with pity and asked me to go home after briefing the team. It was only when I was with the creative team that I noticed the throbbing pain and went to clean my wound. I had the energy to work until very late that night, and for many nights after that, the client's inane request long forgotten.

Very soon after this incident, less than a year after I had joined Leo Burnett, a freelance art director, whose husband was Client Services Director at Ogilvy & Mather, told me that he was looking for an account manager on BMW Asia Pacific and Nokia Southeast Asia. He had interviewed several candidates but had not found anyone suitable. The art director must have heard about my fits of temper and knew about my wounded hand, yet she thought I would make a good account manager on her husband's team at the world's top advertising agency. Within days, I interviewed for the position and a few weeks later, after another round of interviews with the managing director and creative director, I was offered a job as account manager.

Five years after keenly interviewing at various agencies for my first job in advertising, five years after writing to Ogilvy & Mather with an offer they could not refuse but did, I found myself in the hallowed halls of the world's number one advertising agency, handling a multi-million dollar business spanning twenty-two countries in Asia Pacific. For the first time in my life, I understood what it felt like to 'have arrived'.

Ogilvy & Mather, more affectionately known as O&M, was great fun, much like it was at DMB&B and Leo Burnett. By nature of the industry, advertising attracts people with a sense of fun. Even the strange, broody creative types are inclined towards a little fun. I was so glad for the change from fast food to fast cars and a fast-growing industry at the time – the cellular phone.

My first day at O&M was spent poring through several pages of work in progress reports. There was a lot of work that had been suspended while waiting for a new account manager. Now that I had been hired, I had to make up for the agency's and clients' lost time. I had two main print campaigns to launch at the same time, both urgent – the new BMW 7 series in about ten countries in Asia Pacific and the Nokia 2110, one of the smallest GSM phones at the time, in five Southeast Asian countries.

The long hours continued but it was worse for me because the commute was much longer. At O&M, commuting time was around forty-five minutes, twice as long as when I was at the previous agencies. Getting home was sometimes more stressful than the workday itself. The girls went to bed by seven thirty; I usually never made it home before eight or nine. I felt guilty about not spending time with them but the need to prove myself at O&M became a priority. I made an effort to leave the office earlier when Bob was away, but as long as he was home with them, I worked late. It affected the relationship; we began to drift apart and Bob cemented bonds with the girls.

I worked with some very bright and creative people within the agency. My team was small, which made the support role more important. There was something about the secretary in my team which just riled me. I could not put a finger on it but I simmered every time I walked past her desk. She vexed me to the core. Within a month, I experienced my first manic rage at O&M. I screamed at the secretary. I do not remember the reason nor what I said, but she resigned soon after.

In the next eight to ten months, a disproportionate number of secretaries and account executives that my boss hired would either resign or get fired at my urging.

'You're too intolerant,' Bob said when we discussed it one evening at dinner. 'You just can't keep firing people. How bad can they be? Incompetence in aviation means people die. Only the best pilots get to stay. But secretaries? Account executives? Come on, Mahita, cut them some slack.'

'Why should I? Their incompetence means I have to pick up the slack. I don't get the support I need. Clients feel shortchanged. Besides, people like that make me very angry and I don't like losing control. So while it's not drastic, I don't see why I have to put up with it and have them bring out the worst in me when I work in one of the best agencies. If it's the people who make it as good as it is, then we need good people. I can't see why O&M should find it hard to hire good people and fire not-so-good people,' I said.

In due course, a colleague in the Traffic Department started calling me Murphy Brown after Candice Bergen's eponymous character in the hit television show that was still running at the time. Murphy Brown's assistants kept changing to the extent that the resignations became entertainment in itself and other stars played the assistants. Sadly, I did not get the likes of John F Kennedy Jr., Bette Midler or Rosie O'Donnell on my team. I should be so lucky. Eventually, I did put together a small team who worked well together. No one got fired and no one resigned. Still, they insisted on calling me Murphy Brown. Never Murphy, always Murphy Brown. It did not bother me and as it was said in jest, I grew to like it.

* * *

One of my finest moments in advertising was the completion of the BMW 5 Series marketing manual for Asia Pacific in 1996.

This happened almost a year after the launch of the new BMW 7 Series. The new 5 Series, launched around the mid-Nineties, featured many significant changes from design to engineering. Major markets like North America and England were producing their own marketing manuals for their distributors and dealers. The client decided we needed a manual written specifically for the Asia Pacific market but did not have the budget to incur design, copywriting and high production charges. At the same time, he wanted the manual to be in keeping with BMW's high standards of luxury. We eventually agreed that it was essentially a handbook to be used internally so it had to be easy to read and follow. It did not need to be leather-bound and gold-stamped. To keep costs to a minimum, I was given the task of writing the manual and recommending the images for the various chapters.

The client handed me a thick, heavy folder of what must have been third-generation photocopies of badly translated brochures and technical specifications. With that as a resource, O&M was supposed to produce a manual for all twenty-two countries, stretching from India and Sri Lanka to Fiji and Tahiti, managed by the Asia Pacific headquarters of the company that produced the ultimate driving machine. Rather than being intimidated by the prospect, I relished the challenge.

After six weeks of working on the manual, with clear direction from my boss at the very beginning and a couple of sections written by him, along with technical details explained in simpler terms by my technically minded husband Bob, I was almost done. A new account executive had just been hired and together we produced a manual that quickly became every Asia Pacific distributor's essential marketing tool for the new BMW 5 Series launched in 1996.

Delivering the manual to the client's office and seeing his beaming face as he leafed through the pages was a monumental achievement for me on a very personal level. I still had distinct memories of being told that if I continued with my lofty thoughts and strange behaviour, I would amount to nothing. I thought to myself that nothingness could never produce such swish manuals that make technical information sexy. Feeling vindicated, I wanted to shout out loud to Madam Tan a most juvenile 'Screw you!' But I did not. Instead, I remained composed and watched as my German client went slowly through the manual, page by page, smiling.

A year or so after my entrance into the world of O&M, Bob's schedules started to change. He was working considerably more and to make things worse, he was away for several weekends in a row. He had been on the Boeing 747s for several years and his schedule was usually well spread out with a good mix of long-haul and short-haul trips with minimum rest days in between, including weekends. By now some of his flights stretched for as long as two weeks, especially if he also flew the cargo jets. At one point, he was away for thirteen Sundays within four months.

Drained from working long hours during the week, I found it incredibly hard to cope with our young and energetic twins on my own when the helper was off from dawn to dusk. After several years of working long hours all week and spending my time with the family on weekends, I was isolated from my friends. Bob's family lived abroad and mine was in America. I found myself alone, envying my colleagues for the support system they had from their extended families. The girls were around four or five years old, lovely little children, full of spirit so I never felt lonely, but I did feel as if all my energy and drive had dissipated. None of the mothers wanted play dates for their children on Sundays because the fathers were home and wanted to spend time with their families. The girls fought a lot when left to play together. They needed constant supervision and expected to be entertained. I never succumbed to the urge of using the television as a babysitter. That meant having to pursue any activity including storytelling, play acting, going to the zoo or for a drive to yet another playground. I enjoyed doing these with the girls but it got tiring sometimes, especially on oppressively hot and humid days. I understood their demands, more so when they only got to spend time with me mainly on weekends. I found it was getting harder to function after working twelve-hour days virtually all week. Thankfully, Bob's job meant that he was often home during the week; while other fathers were at work, he was able to spend time with the children. When Bob took the children to birthday parties for their kindergarten friends, the mothers and helpers who were there assumed he was a single parent.

I was starting to feel increasingly weak and tired. Well-meaning colleagues said I was anaemic and suggested the most revolting idea of adding chicken liver to my diet. During a lunch with some colleagues, one of them asked if I was all right. Just very, very tired, I said. With genuine concern, she took hold of my hand and said she felt as if the fire had burned out of me. I had not felt it but now that it was mentioned, I knew what she meant. I had not been the same for weeks.

'I've been through this before. It's either stress or exhaustion. Probably both. There's nothing wrong with me, really. I just need some rest but weekends are tough with two young children,' I said.

One day, when the girls were about five, I flew into a rage over their attempts at what I should have recognised as creativity. They had taken a few rolls of toilet paper from their bathroom and wrapped it around their bed frames and side table, covering every bit of wood. Their originality was completely lost on me and instead of being a proud and supportive mother, I went berserk.

'What the fuck is this? Do you not have better things to do, you little shits? Why would you waste loo paper? What was going through your stupid little heads when you decided to do this? Hmm? What?' I screamed as I stood at the doorway.

Even in my crazed state, I noticed the fear in the girls' faces and how they quickly huddled, squatting on their haunches as young children often do, side by side, against the bedroom window which was across the room from me. Caroline had her small hands cupped over her ears and was crying. Elena put her little arms protectively around Caroline's shoulders, heaving along with her sobs, and stared at the floor. That vision of them looking so precious and so vulnerable is etched in my memory. I remember thinking I must stop yelling. But I did not stop. I could not stop.

I went to my room, lay on my bed and started to cry. I was horrified at what I had said and done to the children. I hated myself for being a very bad mother. Why could I not stop? My children needed a better mother. I wished myself dead so Bob could find a new wife who would be a good and kind mother to the girls. I decided I would make it up to them at dinnertime and again at bedtime.

'Toasted cheese! Yummy!' Caroline said and did a child's version of a rain dance.

'Daddy said toasted cheese is only for lunch,' Elena said and promptly joined her sister in a brief rain dance.

'Yes, Daddy's right but it's okay to have it for dinner every now and then. Look, I've cut them out in teddy bear and star shapes for you. But you must also eat the remnants. No wasting food!' I said as I sat down to eat with them at the kitchen table.

After dinner, I got the girls bathed and dressed for bed.

'It's Rapunzel show time today!' I announced as they were

getting into their beds.

'Yippee!' They clapped in unison. I proceeded to play the part of the prince calling out to Rapunzel and asking her to let down her hair. I then grabbed Caroline's blanket, and bunching it on one end, held it at the back of my neck and turned into Rapunzel. They were familiar with the routine but enjoyed it each time. After a few minutes, Rapunzel went to kiss Caroline and then Elena, goodnight.

'Sorry we made you angry, Mama,' said Caroline.

'Sorry, Mama,' repeated Elena.

'Oh, my babies! I am the one who should be sorry. I should never have yelled at you. What you did was art. And even if I did not think it was, I should never have screamed at you and used such bad, bad words. I was worse than Cinderella's wicked stepmother and sisters put together. I am so sorry,' I said, holding back the tears. 'I really don't want to be a bad mummy. I am just so tired. I need to sleep for six months, like a big Mama Bear, and I will be all right. But I can't because I am not a bear. I will try to be good, okay? Promise,' I said and drew them both into my arms, squeezing them tightly and smelling the sweetness in their hair.

'You are a good mummy,' Caroline said and Elena nodded. The kindness on their faces touched me deeply. I smiled at them, glad for their innocence and marvelling at children's ability to forgive so readily.

'Goodnight my sweet, sweet princesses. Sleep tight. I love

you very, very much,' I said as they got into bed. I kissed their foreheads and gave them the usual countdown. 'Two more days and Daddy will be home! Yay! Nighty night. Love you,' I said as I switched off the light and closed the door.

There were too many Sundays like this and when they happened it was always the same – a seemingly calm or extremely happy and fun day, then later in the afternoon suddenly screaming blue murder like a raving lunatic, then putting them to bed, all love and affection, and at night before I went to sleep, the reflection.

Through all those temper tantrums and outbursts, I would look back and be filled with self-loathing for losing control. I tried so hard but just could not stop. I hated myself for being weak, for not being able to control myself. I could not stop even when it cut me to pieces to see my angelic child huddled in a corner, covering her ears, crying, repeating, 'Please don't scream, Mama. Please stop. Please.' This never happened when Bob was around. When he was home, he kept the children company while I took a long nap. I felt more calm and in control. That night, I wished he was home. I prayed hard on those weekend nights without Bob, before going to bed. I prayed for only one thing – to be a better mother. The same prayer, after every full day spent on my own with my children. Nothing good seemed to come of those prayers.

I could feel something was about to happen to me. I could not explain it; I certainly could not understand the feelings and the things going on in my head even though they were all familiar.

I knew something bad was coming my way and I was afraid I would not be prepared. How would I prepare myself anyway? Sitting around waiting for a personal calamity was certainly not going to help. I recognised it as the kind of bad I had experienced before from the weepiness, the thoughts of jumping off a high-rise building and the feeling of being bolted to my bed. It was not a strange feeling, but I did not know what was going to happen nor how nor when. Was I going to fall hard? Was it going to hurt?

One evening, exhausted after a week of working until nearly ten o'clock every night, I went to the multistorey carpark – I sometimes drove to work when Bob was flying – put my bag in the car, walked to the restraining wall and looked out, wondering what it would be like to jump eight high floors down onto solid tarmac below with nothing to break my fall. Would it be very messy? Would my bones shatter? What if someone walked past? I would kill that person, which would be wrong, and worse, I may survive because he would have broken my fall. I would have to go to where the area is closed to pedestrians. I did not think these were bad or wrong thoughts. They were merely thoughts. I felt very tired and wanted to sleep so I got into the car, turned up the music and headed home. Elmer Bernstein's 'Magnificent Seven' had just started playing on the radio and as it was used in the Marlboro commercials for a long time it took me back to those carefree days when Sue and I were at the beach smoking and drinking when we weren't supposed to. Five minutes of happy thoughts to a soundtrack made the drive home that much better.

A few days later I took two days off, my first sick leave at O&M, during which I drove to Toa Payoh one afternoon. I felt too morose to face colleagues and clients. I went to Toa Payoh, one of Singapore's oldest public housing estates which happened to be closest to my home, parked the car near the library, walked to McDonald's and bought a strawberry sundae with extra topping. Although ice cream has been my comfort food of choice since that day in Hong Kong when I was very sad, this time I just felt like having an ice cream. I was not feeling particularly sad.

With the strawberry sundae in hand, I crossed Toa Payoh Central. As I stood on the central divider, waiting for traffic on the other side to clear, my mind was blank, processing nothing, just watching the cars as they drove by. When I reached the block of flats, I threw my now empty plastic sundae cup into the bin and took the lift up to the top floor. I looked below, just as I had done several times since my early twenties. I was not profoundly sad and I certainly was not despondent. I was not running away from a troubled life. I simply had this overwhelming urge to die and simply assumed it was normal. I did not jump because at that very moment, I did not feel like dying. I truly believed many people felt the same way about dying or changing their minds; it's just that some things are too embarrassing or stupid to discuss openly. Some people try to kill themselves and maybe fail or succeed and most people probably don't even bother. It never crossed my mind that it was not normal to *want* to die. Especially when I knew, during my better moments, I had so much to live for.

A week later, eighteen months after I had joined my dream agency, I resigned. It was not something I wanted to do. I just felt I could no longer short-change my husband and children. I could not short-change myself either. I could no longer give all of myself at the office which was the only way I knew to work and have nothing left to give at home. I knew I was going to miss O&M terribly. Ever since I had joined O&M, I had started to define myself by my work. It was at O&M where I learnt that advertising was quite an unforgiving industry but it also gave me back as much as I gave to it. The same was true at DMB&B and also at Leo Burnett but I just did not realise it then. It drained me completely sometimes and then filled me up again. For years I used to feel like the stupid stewardess who dated and then married the clever pilot. My job at O&M reminded me that I was not stupid and gave me the reassurance I so badly needed.

O&M's Group Managing Director at the time was John O'Shea, a very bright and engaging Australian man of about my age. When he heard I had resigned that morning, he called me into his office.

'You resigned today. What's going on?' he asked. I felt slightly intimidated, his eyes looking straight into mine.

'I've been working late ever since I joined O&M. I don't think it is poor time management. There is just so much to do. It doesn't help that I am really into detail,' I said. 'It's affecting me, which in turn affects my family. Bob's away a lot, which makes it harder. I simply cannot cope, watching my domestic life collapse around me. I am merely existing, John. Sometimes I feel I am cracking up.'

'Would it help if you worked shorter hours?' he asked. He was half-smiling. I wondered if he had a plan.

'Of course it would but clients already expect so much, how would I manage, realistically?' I asked.

'That would be my problem. Leave it to me. I suggest you work on the Nokia account because it involves fewer markets. Let's try 9 a.m. to 1 p.m. for a few months. I'll talk to the client and explain that it is just a matter of time management and that he will still get full support from the account executive in the afternoon. You'll just need to be flexible and go for afternoon meetings if that's the only available time for the Nokia team.'

We agreed we would try this out for three to six months. O&M was always a trailblazer in the frantic advertising industry and John O'Shea as head of the Singapore office had just created what was quite possibly the country's first part-time client-servicing position in an international agency. It took several years before other big agencies caught on to the practice.

I felt very special to have the world's number one agency customise a position to suit my needs while there was a long line of perfectly capable managers waiting to take my place and work long hours. It was a privilege for which I will always be grateful to

John. On the bus home that day I thought about my conversation with John and the outcome. I couldn't help but smile to myself. After feeling I had arrived on my first day at O&M, I now felt I was taking off on a supersonic jet with a glass of champagne in my hand. I was valued by the big boss of the top advertising agency. A special arrangement was made to accommodate my need for reduced hours. For the very first time, I felt truly successful.

After four months of working for half pay and leaving the office at around four in the afternoon instead of one o'clock, I quit for the second time. The arrangement was simply not going to work without the support of my day-to-day contact at Nokia who, it seemed to me, did not even try to hide his resentment as soon as he was told about my reduced working hours.

Some months later, Valerie, a colleague from a different division at O&M, called to offer me another part-time position, the first of many she would offer me over the next three years. This was for a project with IBM. I worked until one in the afternoon for seven months. The client and the agency were equally supportive and respectful of my hours. I was happy and calm and for the first time in many years I felt a sense of peace descend upon me. I did not feel restless during those seven months. I was neither particularly energetic nor was I tired, angry or sad. Years later when I looked back at the various phases in my life, those seven months which I refer to as my IBM phase, were probably the closest I had come to being a normal person in about twenty years. Or so I thought.

Working half days meant more time for indulgences like beauty care. I signed up for facial and nail care packages at various places. They were very expensive and I did not think about how much more I was spending now that I had so much less to spend. On top of these fortnightly treatments, I bought preparations to supplement my routine at home. These included face masks and cuticle cream at insane prices, all justified by words like 'Professional Care', 'Expert Treatment'. I bought enough to last me a year. I even bought ten bottles of Clarins cellulite lotion when I hardly had any to remove. I never used any of them and threw the unopened bottles two years later while clearing out my cupboard.

When I saw my credit card bill for that month, I knew I could not renew the packages or buy specialty treatments again. I could not afford them and did not think it was fair to ask Bob to fund such frivolous afternoons at the salon. Until then, I still had five months of treatments paid for so I continued with them until they were all redeemed.

Just before the end of those seven months, on a happy afternoon while Bob, the girls and I were playing a lively game of Uno in the living room, I received a courier package. It was a four-page letter written entirely in Chinese from Guangzhou, China. I ran barefoot to a neighbour's apartment on the third floor.

'Uncle Lim, please help me. I have a letter from China,

from my Amah! Please help me to read it,' I was trembling with excitement. After years of sending letters every six months with the help of friends who could write in Chinese, I finally got a response. I was thankful to the girls' Chinese tutor who suggested addressing my letter to the district town council's office.

He scanned all three pages before translating the contents.

'I think this is going to make you very sad but there are also some good things here, I will translate the overall letter, not word for word. The language is very old-fashioned and flowery,' he said. My face suddenly felt hot and wet. The tears flowed freely. I had not expected Amah to still be alive but I always remained hopeful. Uncle Lim continued 'Greetings Mrs Mahita! I am Go Go, your elder brother, your Amah's son. My family was very happy to get a letter from you. We saw the stamp and calculated that it took six months to reach even by airmail. You said you sent many letters. We did not get any. I think we received this letter because you sent it to a government office. My mother gave you the wrong address. I am sorry to tell you that your Amah passed away in 1987. She became senile and very sick but had a peaceful death ...'

'Stop! Uncle Lim, this is more than I can bear. I'll come back another day for the rest of the letter. Thank you Uncle Lim,' I said and stretched out my hand for the letter.

'She thought of you every day, according to the letter,' said Uncle Lim as he folded the letter and handed it to me. I nodded and thanked him again.

I ran up the fire exit and burst through the door.

'She died in 1987, Bob! Ten years ago! She's gone,' I said, still in tears. I went to our room and cried while the girls offered me comfort with hugs and kisses.

'I was not allowed into China while she was alive and I never heard from her or her family. I must at least honour Amah in death,' I said to Bob during dinner that evening. 'I'll go for Qing Ming. It's usually in early April, six months away, so I'll go to China next year, just for a long weekend.'

'Just check with her family that it's okay for you to go. They might want it to be private,' Bob said. 'By the way, Singapore Airlines now flies to several cities in China, ever since the Singapore government raised travel restrictions a couple of years ago. I'll get you a ticket but first confirm that you won't be intruding.'

With the right address, correspondence became easier. I flew to China and met Amah's family – they were my family too, Go Go said – on Good Friday, 1998. The following day we went to Amah's gravesite where I swept and weeded her grave and made offerings of fruit and confectionery. I spoke to her while sweeping and weeding her semi-circular grave. Her son's family watched me sympathetically.

'Amah, forgive me for breaking my promise to see you. I have thought of you every day since you left Singapore. I wrote letters you never received. I married a good man, Amah. We have twin girls and we celebrate Chinese New Year and the Lantern Festival every year. Ever since the babies came,' I stopped sweeping and started to cry. After a few moments, I resumed sweeping and the one-way conversation. 'We always have a reunion dinner on New Year's Eve. The next day we give the girls *hong bao* – not a lot, just $8 – but they're always happy. And like you used to do with me, I take them to the playground on Lantern night in their pyjamas and they parade with the other kids holding their candle-lit lanterns. I do all this in honour of you.' It was a very emotional experience but rewarding at the same time, helping me come to terms with her death and greatly easing my guilt. *I will come back again, my beloved Amah. Rest in peace.*

* * *

Thanks to Valerie, my colleague initially and later my boss who eventually became a dear friend, I was never short of jobs at O&M. For the next few years, I went in and out of O&M on various part-time positions including projects for American Express. As usual, I poured myself completely into my work while at the office, but all within very sensible hours. Spending more time at home meant noticing the ineptitude of the various live-in helpers. This resulted in helpers walking through my front door more frequently than I did at O&M. In the first year I started working part-time, we had a reasonably good helper and I was able to keep my emotions in check at home. In the second year, we hired, in sequence, at least six Filipina live-in helpers amongst whom was a part-time prostitute who plied her trade at her lover's condominium between the wee hours of two and six in the morning, a pretty mother of three with a string of eager admirers from a contingent of Bangladeshi construction workers who called at all hours, two thieves and a lovely young woman with much enthusiasm and no common sense.

I was at my wits' end. Instead of spending more time with my husband, I was pushing him away with my outbursts at all these women. They were all hired out of desperation, without paying any attention to my instinct. With most of the helpers that did not work out, I had a gut feeling while interviewing them that something was not quite right. With each interview, however, I forgot my past experience with rogue helpers and hired the first available helper who could cook and take care of young children.

The slightest provocation set me off on frenzied screaming and swearing. A helper gave Caroline her steroid inhaler two hours after her last dose even though I had written clearly 'every six hours'. Another helper washed an expensive dress when she was told it had to be dry-cleaned. Yet another helper soaked all twenty of my miniature Swarovski crystal animals in hot soapy water; they were sparkling clean but all the bits and pieces that were glued – birds' beaks and wings, other animals' legs and tails – had washed off. Most were salvaged but I had to take them to Swarovski to get them fixed. Yet another helper burnt Elena's favourite t-shirt with an iron that was too hot. With every incident, I ranted and raved. I threw things and left trails of destruction. I then called yet another agent for yet another replacement. I never laid a finger on any of them but there were several instances when I wanted to hit them with whatever was close at hand. Instead, I aimed at the floor and threw whatever I laid my hand on.

If it wasn't work I could blame, it was the helper and if it wasn't her, it was the kids. I never thought it was anything to do with me.

I did not want to keep transforming into and out of this monstrous persona. It was exhausting and confusing, but I did not know how to be anyone else. I continued to blame stress, everyone's favourite punching bag to which both serious and frivolous ailments as well as behavioural disorders are unfairly attributed.

By now, Bob, my long-suffering husband, not knowing how to deal with the senseless shouting, had withdrawn to the point where there was a distance between us yet at the same time we had a very close bond because of our children.

* * *

After one of my projects at Ogilvy, I was offered a three-month stint at another leading agency, Batey, to assist in the launch of

Starhub, Singapore's third telecommunications company. As an account director, I worked alongside another account director who was transitioning from her existing account to Starhub. The demands from the client and within the agency itself were great. The hours were very long but I felt motivated and happy on most days. Batey was a vibrant agency with strong creative and energetic client-servicing teams. I had the energy to work until ten or eleven every night and start at eight o'clock the next morning.

I was offered a permanent position at Batey on another account and while I was keen to continue working at Batey for the work and the environment, I was not ready for such long hours with no end in sight. After my three months were up, I went back to O&M on yet another part-time position for American Express. While at O&M, a very dear friend, Alison, called to tell me about a job opportunity. She was a former colleague who had become a close family friend, and was running her own design agency. Upon hearing that one of her clients was looking to fill a position, she immediately thought of me.

After nearly ten years in advertising, I looked forward to what I thought was the best job in the world. I enjoyed the roller-coaster world of advertising, but was now ready to leave it behind for a more stable environment.

Little did I know that the wild ride was always in my head and that the roller-coaster would follow me everywhere.

CHAPTER 5

'On a bad day I have mood swings – but on a good day,
I have the whole mood playground.'
Charles Rosenblum

When Alison first called to tell me about this position, she knew the job scope was too small for me, but emailed me the job requirements anyway, thinking the prospect of working for the world's top luxury hotel company would make up for the smaller title and pay. I was sure it was going to be too easy, taking me back to where I was about eight years before. I was concerned it might be a little too boring for me, but Alison convinced me that it was a totally different kind of company and I would love it just for the people and the environment.

Within a week, I was called for an interview. In the first five minutes of meeting Jonathan Sicroff, the Vice President, Sales and Marketing, I was hooked. He was clearly very smart, funny, well-groomed and seemed genuinely nice. I liked him right away and wanted to work with him. He told me he was interviewing several candidates. The competition made me want the job even more. I prayed for the next interview. I got that second interview but it gave me second thoughts. I sensed the interviewer did not like me. After that session, my enthusiasm waned.

A couple of weeks later, I was called for a third interview. By then, I thought it didn't matter whether or not I got this job. The third interview was with Neil Jacobs, Regional Vice President and General Manager of Four Seasons Hotel Singapore and the most senior Four Seasons hotelier in Asia Pacific at that time. He was very warm and welcoming, but he also seemed in a hurry. The interview lasted five minutes. I was miffed due to the time spent preparing for the interview and dressing up with emphasis on grooming, especially as I was not the full make-up and manicure type.

I called Bob from outside, near the hotel's taxi rank. He was surprised to hear from me so quickly.

'I think I blew it,' I said and started to cry. I can cry easily but not over something as trivial as not getting what I want, jobs and jewellery included. But this was different; I had swung so quickly from nonchalance following my second interview to desperately wanting *this* job. The attraction was in working with Jonathan Sicroff and Neil Jacobs in an environment that could only have been created by the world's leading luxury hospitality company. I wanted to wear nice clothes and surround myself with splendour. I wanted to work for Four Seasons for all it symbolised, regardless of the job itself. I knew I would be very good at what I did. My bosses and peers would see it in a matter of weeks, maybe even days.

I kept replaying the scene with Neil Jacobs in my head, my shortest interview ever. Perhaps I was overconfident. Mr Jacobs expressed concern that I did not have hotel experience. I expressed surprise that it was even necessary, considering I was being hired for communications and had solid experience in the world's leading communications company. Perhaps I came across as disrespectful to a person clearly accustomed to being fawned. Perhaps I had offended him.

Having given up hope, I was delighted when ten days later, during a quiet afternoon at home, Jonathan's secretary called to arrange a telephone interview with the Senior Vice President for Marketing at Four Seasons headquarters in Toronto. That was to be my fourth and last interview. After the brief session with Neil Jacobs, this came as a big and very pleasant surprise.

As with Jonathan and Neil, Susan Helstab was immensely warm and kind. After more than ten years in advertising, working mainly on brands which were industry leaders globally, I had never met a single client who embodied his or her company's philosophy the way people at Four Seasons did. Everyone I had met so far was a walking, breathing statement of luxury hospitality. I do not remember how long the interview took but I remember it was nearly ten o'clock at night in Singapore, and although it was nearly my bedtime, I was feeling wide awake and comfortable right away with not a nervous muscle twitching in my body.

A few days later, Jonathan called and made me an offer I could have easily refused – the pay was insultingly low – but I wanted to be at Four Seasons so much I was not going to let a few thousand dollars a month get in the way.

'You're out of your mind, Mahita! It's a huge pay cut. It's only a bit more than what you were getting at O&M working half days and being home a lot with the children. I don't think you should be shortchanging yourself to such an extent,' said Bob.

'It's okay, Bob. We'll manage as we have been doing until now. I have a really good feeling about this job and it's all because of the people. I never knew what corporate culture meant until my first meeting with Jonathan. The environment means a lot to me, Bob. Please understand,' I said. 'It's a big cut but a small price to pay for a dream job. I can't deal with stress, you've said so enough times. This will be perfect. Besides, it is an adequate salary for the position. I'm just overqualified. Plus I get to go to Toronto twice a year, each time for a week at a stretch. That would be fun. I can see my mother in the U.S. on the way there or back.'

Bob was not entirely convinced but he agreed it was worth a shot knowing I could always go back to part-time work at O&M.

I called Jonathan the next day and said yes please, thank you and when do I start?

On my thirty-seventh birthday, I resigned from O&M, signed yet another employment contract and was all set to work at Four

Seasons Hotels and Resorts. I had to pinch myself to believe I had just been hired by the world's number one luxury hotel company.

Three months into my new job, I was sent to the company's headquarters in Toronto. My schedule allowed a free weekend in between. I called Sue before I left Singapore and she arranged to meet me at the Four Seasons Hotel in Toronto. We spent the night in my room and drove to her home in Michigan the next day. I met her husband and two sons. We enjoyed a lovely dinner of barbecued ribs then stayed up late into the night chatting and looking at old photographs. Time flew by all too quickly and on Sunday evening Sue drove me to Detroit where I caught the train back to Toronto. I was extremely happy that weekend and planned to make a weekend with Sue an annual event. Sadly, by the time I next visited Toronto, Sue had moved to Texas.

At work, the first year was a heady mix of introducing new initiatives for a market just crawling out of the 1997 Asian financial crisis, a debacle that raised fears of a global economic meltdown. I worked on building relationships with general managers and directors of marketing. I reported to Jonathan and enjoyed every moment working with him.

Jonathan realised very early on that I was starting to get bored and was hungry for more. He involved me in his work, improving the situation and allowing me to venture beyond just communications and into the sales and marketing side. Thanks to Jonathan, my job became much more stimulating and enjoyable.

At the end of my first year, he gave me a very good review and a substantial raise.

Although I wanted stability, I started to miss the vibrant agency environment. There was a long stretch where, for about three or four months, I did not experience bursts of energy and creativity or find myself in stimulating conversations with people or feel invincible. I missed all that but was at the same time I was thankful for not finding myself in situations where I lashed out at someone in a fiery rage. I was grateful for the sensible hours which allowed me to enjoy a couple of hours with the girls and before they went to bed. Bob commented that I seemed happier and more relaxed. Those times felt like my IBM phase from a few years earlier at O&M, but not quite.

Although I was very happy at Four Seasons, I felt empty inside. I thought maybe it was due to the work being too easy, which it was, but I liked it because of the environment and I rarely had to work weekends and long hours. Watching Bob and the girls happily playing a board game on Sunday afternoon, I felt my tears welling up. I announced I was going to take a nap.

Lying in bed, I thought about how far Bob and I had drifted apart. I desperately wanted to be happy and I wanted to make Bob happy. I knew he was unhappy too; it cannot be easy for a calm person like Bob to be married to a temperamental person like me. I thought about my options and while I considered a divorce, I wondered at the same time about trying to be a better wife. There was also the popular option favoured by unhappy couples all over the world, the one where we would stay together and pretend everything was fine until the kids left for university. Eventually I decided I was too scared to choose and even more scared to disrupt the children's stable, sheltered lives. Uncertain of what the future held, and afraid of being alone, I opted for the status quo. We were, after all, a very close family.

Two years after I joined Four Seasons, in the autumn of 2001, Jonathan relocated to North America. I was devastated. Jonathan fulfilled all my professional needs, and within the framework of the job, my personal needs too. Now he was returning to America. I was happy for him, but felt abandoned and allowed myself to wallow in self-pity.

With the arrival of my new boss, Paul, the organisation structure for Marketing in the Asia Pacific office changed, but it was several months before the new structure was implemented. I had three bosses: Paul and two others, Beth and Dave, in Toronto. I did not see a problem at first but soon it was evident my job had shrunk from a role requiring some thinking to one that largely involved taking and passing on orders.

Soon after the reduction in my job responsibility, the downward spiral began – slowly at first and very rapidly all of a sudden.

* * *

Things were better at home; the children were sleeping thirty minutes later on school nights and I treasured that extra time with them. Bob and I were still very close because of the children.

Between early 2002 and mid-2003, after struggling to come to terms with my reduced role at work, I managed to enjoy several long phases of relative calm. Paul allowed me to help him with small sections of his work which made some of my days more interesting. At home, a new helper joined us and within weeks proved the best we ever had, leagues above her thirteen predecessors. It made a remarkable difference to the atmosphere at home. Ani planned the menus, did the shopping for food and ensured we were well looked after. As I had to travel occasionally while Bob was on a flight, Ani took the girls to all their activities, borrowed books for them from the library, ensured they did their homework and kept them entertained. She was Nanny McPhee and Martha Stewart in one. Not once did she ever set me off, unlike the many helpers before her.

I started to pray every night. I always said a teaspoon prayer, 'tsp' just like in the recipe books – thank you, sorry, please. Thank you was usually the same. I thanked God for all his blessings because no matter how badly I felt inside, I had two fabulous children, a decent husband, a secure home, a good job and a few good friends. Sorry varied depending on the day. I said sorry for anything I thought I did wrong including screaming at someone, being a bad mother, gossiping or refusing to lend a known gambler the hundred dollars he asked for, claiming he needed to buy food. The please part was when I got greedy. I asked for a lot but not always at the same time. I always prayed for my children's health. I always asked for happiness and peace in my heart and for a mind that would cooperate and be calm most of the time. I prayed for a friend who had a dying parent. I asked for various things at various times. I often asked for a promotion. As my life was good in every material sense, I came to believe in a God I was sure of.

* * *

There were many photoshoots for various hotels scheduled for the next six months. I usually had boundless energy for these sessions which often meant working all day and all night, combined with day-to-day emails that still needed to be read and answered, and shooting at four or five in the morning to catch that magic light just before the break of day. What was noticeably missing for me now was that magical feeling of invincibility.

Starting around the end of 2003, there were weeks on end when I was talkative, bursting with energy and writing creatively. I was prone to shopping sprees at the mall next door. I bought things I did not need and never used, from rings and necklaces to toiletries and stationery. After that, there would be a week or so when it was quite the opposite. I experienced the wretched cycle of rage and energy followed by that debilitating sadness that had tortured me before. I decided it was just a natural life cycle, just like feeling sick after overeating – anyone who feels extremely happy for a few weeks, will inevitably feel extremely sad after a while. I figured it was the body and mind's natural mechanism for ensuring people get the break they needed. Convinced my theory was logical, I did not give my feelings much thought.

I don't know when it happened or how, but even on my best days I was only half as exuberant or motivated as I used to be. I was not much fun to myself. Although I noticed it, I was too busy and distracted to analyse it. Somewhere along the way, I had lost a side of me I really liked.

Beth, one of my two bosses in Toronto, tried to attend as many photoshoots as she could squeeze into her tight schedule. Due to the distance combined with the number of hotels in Europe which required photo-shoots at the same time, Beth could not always be in Asia. As much as I liked her as a person, with all my respect and affection for her, I started to resent her as a boss. Still, she was great company and very kind. On the last day of a pre-opening shoot for Four Seasons Hotel Hong Kong, fed up with being the gofer in what I saw as pretentious creativity masquerading as dedication to an art form, I barged onto the set, hauled the props in and yelled.

'Here! Take these fucking props and create your fucking fake room. If you think these aren't good enough for your dated over-the-top set-ups, go get your own props!' I knew I was angry but had not realised I was yelling at my boss. Beth was shocked, but said nothing and looked at me, waiting for me to stop. Later that evening, back at the hotel, Beth spoke to me and tried to make sense of why I reacted the way I did. I could not explain it and could only apologise profusely through free-flowing tears. The next morning we carried on as if nothing had happened. It helped that Beth appeared to have put the episode behind us.

Weeks later, at a pre-opening shoot at Four Seasons Resort Langkawi, I had an altercation over equipment storage with the photographer's assistant, a gentle, soft-spoken young man from Thailand.

'Excuse me! What do you think you are doing? The shoot isn't over! Why the fuck are you putting your equipment away? And did you check if it's okay to keep your things in that room? Did you? Did you?' I yelled across the garden to the assistant about ten feet away.

Again Beth was there and she spoke to me immediately but this time I was not listening to her. As she spoke, my head was spinning out of control, I could feel it. I wanted to say more cruel words, this time aimed at her, accompanied by some swearing now at the tip of my tongue. I wanted to do more, like throw something against a wall. I didn't do anything. I just froze with all this anger inside me; I could feel it, but I could not understand it. It took several minutes before I was able to come to my senses and walk to the car. The shoot ended two days later and life went back to normal for a few weeks.

After the shoot came the collateral design which was done by a Singapore-based design agency appointed partly because I had strongly recommended the designer. As was the usual practice since the restructuring, I had to send everything to Beth, from initial selection of first-round layouts until final approval, including second- or third-round creatives with the most insignificant revisions, such as a word change or a thumbnail image change; it became a long drawn-out process. With my delicate frame of mind at that time, the insignificance of my job resulted in noticeably more frequent and intense outbursts I could not control.

The unfortunate recipient of my rabid yelling was one of the agency designers. One day, after he refused to make a change I had requested, preferring instead to get Beth's input first, I went berserk and screamed down the telephone.

'Listen, I don't know what games you're playing but don't ever forget who got you to where you are now. When things did not work out at the last agency, you asked me about starting your own agency. Remember? I was the one who believed you were talented and supported you,' I said, almost tasting the venom at the tip of my tongue but unable to stop. 'Without me, the bosses in Toronto would never have given you the time of day. You owe me big time. Get that? Big fucking time! You may think you're Mr Big Shot but you are nothing but a small, small man.' I slammed the receiver and yelled 'Fuck you!' into the phone, oblivious to the impact of my high-octane diatribes on my soft-spoken and gentle colleagues who signed up for working in the happy, cosy environment that Four Seasons promised. Just as I had done during my first outburst with Beth, I had violated every code of conduct in the company's employee handbook without even realising it. Such a violation was probably grounds for termination so it was providence that all the bosses were away at that time.

As nasty and undignified as my behaviour was, I could not stop. I had the ability to reflect on my words and deeds later when I had calmed down but not the power to stop myself from saying things I should not say.

The next day, while Paul was still away, he called and told me that my flare-ups were having a bad effect on all those around me. In a kind voice and direct words, he asked me to tone it down. It was obvious a colleague had complained to him about the screaming fits. It was the first time since I was in school that someone had asked me to tone down. Only this time, I knew exactly why and what the words meant. I wanted very much to do as Paul asked. I just did not know how.

Several days later, I took a call from Beth who was in Europe at the time. It made a change from the countless late-night calls I had to make during her Toronto morning to chase for approvals. During this call, she said that she still did not like the picture on the television screen. I was speechless. She was referring to a beautiful centre-spread image of a stunning master bedroom looking out to the Andaman Sea framed by imaginative graphics, thumbnail images evocative of the perfect resort getaway. What more could she want? She wanted to change the picture within a television screen, an image that was less than a quarter of an inch square and took up less than one percent of the page. That tiny image had been changed at least three times, and I thought all those options were good. While I appreciated perfectionism, it baffled me that someone with such a big mind could squander so much time and energy on what was to me nothing more than an insignificant change that was unlikely to enhance the end result.

'It's a fucking TV screen for God's sake! The picture is smaller than the nail on my pinkie, even with it chewed down to my finger stub! The woman is insane. I swear she is fucking insane!' I screamed as soon as I hung up. I noticed the pervasive silence. It was deafening. I grabbed my wallet and stormed out of the office, telling Paul's assistant I needed some air.

The sheer monotony of the job I was doing hit me hard that afternoon. I walked to the mall next door and got myself a large strawberry milkshake. With the cold milkshake in my hand, the paper cup quickly damp from condensation, I walked to the courtyard outside The Regent Hotel and sat on one of the uncomfortable wrought-iron chairs. It was late afternoon and still quite hot. My heart was heavy and my mind was still hazy from the conversation with Beth barely fifteen minutes earlier. I watched a stray cat licking itself about ten feet away from me and thought about how I managed to get myself into a role that was far from what I signed up for. The once-promising position had rapidly and unexpectedly diminished into nothing, and I could not deal with the turmoil going on in my heart and my head. I wondered if I was somehow responsible. I tried to make sense of a situation so bizarre it was unimaginable in a company consistently ranked on Fortune's and CNN's list of 100 Best Companies to Work For. What was I missing?

As I walked back to the office, I told myself that I did not struggle all these years, working my way up ladders while battling countless conflicts only to be a co-ordinator seeking approval on a mere brochure from someone who should be no more than my equal. After years of working on high-profile multi-million-dollar campaigns with some of Singapore's best brains in advertising and marketing, I believed I was meant for bigger and better things. Even if my scope of work had never expanded from when I accepted this job working with Jonathan, I never expected it to degenerate into something so mind-numbing and soul-destroying that I felt I was on the verge of losing my mind.

Later that afternoon, with my head clearer and my anger left behind at the courtyard, I sat at my desk and looked at the brochure again. I reviewed Beth's comments, and creativity being subjective, I sincerely believed in my humble opinion that there was not an image that was better because Beth was at a photoshoot, nor a brochure that was better because Beth had approved it.

That night, I did not eat or sleep. I put the girls to bed mechanically, my mind being elsewhere. Bob was away and although I longed to speak to him I did not want to bother him. I did not want him to talk me out of quitting a job that appeared glamorous and interesting on the outside but was sheer drudgery in reality. For months the resentment had been slowly building and in recent weeks it had started messing up my head with an intensity and frequency I had never felt before. I wanted to die. I did not want to be this person.

I was not getting any intellectual stimulation at work, nor any comfort at home with Bob away a lot. I relied entirely on devouring literary fiction and *The Financial Times* as brain food but they were not interactive. I looked forward to my monthly meetings as a committee member at the Society for the Prevention of Cruelty to Animals. While the experiences were rewarding, they were not stimulating enough.

The next morning, as I kissed the girls goodbye on their usual morning dash for the school bus, I told them I was going to resign and would spend more time at home with them. Caroline cried and Elena followed and said no, please don't quit. Please, Mama, don't quit. They had grown quite accustomed to free nights and room service in stunning hotels in Maldives, Bali, Paris and London; they were naturally looking forward to more. Stepping into the opulence of George V Paris and squealing with delight at the floral arrangements before being shown up to the most elegant and ornate room they had ever seen; checking into a two-bedroom villa in Bali Jimbaran Bay with their own bedroom and outdoor shower, cookies iced with their names and kid-size batik robes; their own beachfront villa in Maldives Kuda Huraa. What experiences! Now, it was over. They were only twelve years old and could not possibly understand the extent of my pain and the consequences I would have to bear for staying.

I spoke on the phone to my three bosses that night – Paul who was in Tokyo, Dave in Toronto and Beth who was in Paris, in that order. I sensed that Paul, nice as he was to me while I worked with him and much as I enjoyed the experience, was relieved as he no longer had to deal with a mercurial employee on his team while Dave seemed genuinely saddened by the news. Beth must have seen it coming. Her immediate reaction and first question was quite telling: 'It's not because of me, is it?' I wanted to say yes, Beth, absolutely, because my role was reduced to nothing from the moment I had to report to you and yes, it was entirely because of you, but how could I tell her? On a personal level, she had been very good to me.

'No, Beth, of course not,' I said and wondered if she believed me. I was not angry with her and softened as she asked what brought on the sudden decision. I told her I needed more intellectual stimulation. She realised I was feeling fragile and that I did not really want to quit, but that it was necessary for me.

Beth had an exceptional way with words and with her help that night I drafted the best resignation letter I had ever written. It had the perfect blend of joy, sadness and gratitude. The choice of words and sentence structure made it quite poetic. It also officially removed any suspicion of Beth being the cause of my resignation.

The next morning, in June 2004, I officially resigned from what I truly believed was, at one point, for me, the best job in the world. For the first time, and it remains the only time, I was gripped by grief so acute I never thought possible when resigning from a job. I did not want to leave, but I had to. It was self-preservation without actually thinking about it. I could not even begin to wonder what I was going to do next.

So much for a stable environment. If I did not find it at the end of five years at Four Seasons, I was convinced it did not exist in any company.

CHAPTER 6

'My own brain is to me the most unaccountable of machinery
– always buzzing, humming, soaring, roaring, diving, and then
buried in mud. And why? What's this passion for?'

Virginia Woolf

After a one-month hiatus , during which I co-founded a book club
and did a brief stint at a food consultancy, I was itching to go back
to advertising. I loved the stimulating environment, the sense of
fun, the colourful characters in the creative department, the whole
business of advertising itself and, above all, the pace. Events on
any given day went as slowly or as quickly as was necessary to but
it was never too slow for me.

A headhunter arranged an interview for a position at McCann
Erickson. I was sent to meet Sorab Mistry, the Chief Executive
Officer, who in a few months would become my boss. It was a
strange interview for the position of group business director;
he wanted to know about me as a person. My interests, my
aspirations, my fears. He had my resumé and knew I was qualified
for the job but he wanted to know if I was the right person for

the agency and to head a young team. I knew I wanted to work with this CEO because he was clearly very intelligent and would provide the stimulation I needed when my clients couldn't. More than that, it was because he would always see me as a person, not just an employee or a member of his management committee.

After several weeks, just before Christmas, I was offered the position and so began another phase in my life in the new year of 2005. The position required me to oversee a team of six account executives and managers responsible for a number of accounts, the two most significant being L'Oreal and Tiffany & Co. Both global industry leaders; I was thrilled. I had been a loyal fan of L'Oreal skincare and hair care for nearly five years. I had enjoyed many Holly Golightly moments outside Tiffany's at Raffles Hotel in Singapore. I believed I was perfect for the position.

In less than three months I also became the agency's accidental Business Development Director, after being the only senior person available to attend a briefing for the agency's first pitch of the year, Republic of Singapore Air Force, a prestigious government account. After nearly three years of not having to think at work, I was now required to use every cell in my brain to write marketing and creative strategies. Working with a strong team comprised of people from various departments – Media, Planning, Creative and Client Servicing – we recruited a number of bright young men from the various Defence sections for research on why they chose or did not choose the Air Force, we wrote and re-wrote, a number of times, strategic briefs and pitch documents. We reviewed a number of creative approaches and media buying ideas.

For many of us, fifteen-hour days were the norm. Thankfully the commute for me was less than ten minutes each way. Most evenings, when I locked up, I felt I had run very hard all day but I was not tired. I was happy and needed very little sleep. I felt like I was on a high and was not ready to land. Not just yet.

The day before the Air Force submission, I saw the children off to the school bus in the morning. For several days in a row that week, I was usually asleep when they left for school and they were always in bed when I came home from work. I told them that I would try and be home in time for dinner and then go back to the office to finish my work by midnight. Bob was away so for a few nights they had dinner by themselves in the kitchen. I missed them terribly and was longing for a catch-up even if only over a quick dinner. They were now thirteen years old and at the age where there was so much to say about school and their friends. I did not want to miss out on their lives.

That evening, at about five o'clock, my daughter Caroline called to say that she was at the hospital, with sharp pains in her side. Ani, our Heaven-sent helper, was with her. Elena was home alone. I wanted to drop everything and be with Caroline but the submission deadline was just sixteen hours away and there was a lot still left to do. At this point I was working out costs and budgets and was so deep into the process I could not even think about delegating the work to anyone. Heartbroken, I asked Caroline to keep me posted, to call me if there was anything serious. Two hours later, Ani called from the hospital to say that Caroline was waiting to be admitted. I was very upset for my precious child and promised to see her very soon. She was admitted around ten that night and went to bed straight away. I spoke to the nurse who said it was just for observation and she would be fine. Before I knew it, it was three in the morning. I left the office, went home, got a change of clothes and drove to KK Women's and Children's Hospital. I crawled into the foldaway bed that had been arranged for me. It was nearly four in the morning by then. I had to be up in two hours to get back to the office and take the big submission package, with all the creative boards, to the Air Force office.

At seven in the morning I kissed Caroline's soft, sweet-smelling head and, whispering, told her I would see her soon. An hour later, my colleague and I submitted a huge box of creative concepts and copies of the strategic document and budgets at the Air Force office on Depot Road. We breathed a huge sigh of relief. The first round was over. I had slept for less than three hours over a twenty-six-hour period and I was feeling a little jumpy. I had no idea where all that energy came from. I couldn't remember the last time I was so energised at work. I felt as if I was flying. I did not question what I was feeling because I never thought there was anything wrong with feeling this good and this happy.

An hour later I was back at the hospital to be with Caroline;

the doctor said she would be discharged later that afternoon. Another sigh of relief, this time bigger than the one this morning. I spent the next three hours at Caroline's side, sleeping on the floor. It took me a long time to overcome the guilt of not rushing to her side immediately despite Caroline's assurances that she totally understood why and it did not matter. It mattered to me.

The next few months passed without incident. Eventually we made it to the final shortlist for the Air Force. It was between McCann and the incumbent. The incumbent won. Those of us who gave so much of ourselves were disappointed and tired, but also ready to move on to the next pitch. We knew we had done our best and it was all that mattered.

Several weeks after the end of the big pitch and days before I was due to leave for a two-week family holiday in Europe, one of my clients, Tiffany & Co, had a small, by-invitation-only event at their flagship Orchard Road store. Some of my colleagues and I went as invited guests without any intention of buying jewellery. Within half an hour of arriving at the store, my colleague bought a ring, one of a line of stackable Celebration Rings that Tiffany had recently launched.

'It's for me. I am celebrating me,' she said.

Thinking about what I had to celebrate, I bought the least expensive ring on display. It was a thin band of white gold with a small diamond in the centre and even smaller diamonds to the left and right and stopping halfway down.

'I don't see anything to celebrate about me but I have two fabulous children. This celebrates them,' I said.

'Buy another one. Celebrate your husband! The rings are stackable, I'm sure you know that.'

'Can't afford two rings but this one will cover the family. With this ring, I not only celebrate Bob and the girls, I also pledge to be a better mother and a better wife.' I looked at the tiny sparking diamonds and thought how lucky I was to be part of my family.

* * *

A few days later, I was finishing as much work as possible in preparation for my holiday. I was in my office going through budgets with a young executive for one of the L'Oreal brands. I did some calculations on an Excel file while she watched blankly, with her hand under her chin. Concerned by the vagueness on her face, I asked her if she understood Excel and knew how to add the various entries.

'It's okay. I'll just use a calculator. No problem,' she replied with such nonchalance that I flew off the handle.

'Are you fucking retarded?' I screamed while I grabbed her wrist and glared at her. I screamed at her again, asking the same question. A deathly quiet descended on the corridor outside, and I could see through my window the executives and managers and secretaries all staring at their computers in hushed silence. It was about ten past nine in the morning.

I knew I was totally out of line. After a few seconds staring at the computer screen without actually seeing anything, I breathed deeply and, pulling myself together, said, 'I was out of line. I'm sorry. At twenty-two, you should be teaching me to go beyond the basics in Excel. What I was doing was the basics. If you don't know, learn. Telling me you will use the calculator doesn't just take you back ten years, it says that you're stupid and lazy.' We quickly snapped back into the discussion as if nothing happened. I hadn't experienced this rage in such a long time and had forgotten how quickly it comes and goes. It shook me as I could not see it coming, nor could I control it, just like every single time.

That night during dinner before we left for the airport, I told Bob and the girls what had happened and said that if anyone ever spoke to our daughters in that tone with such harsh words, they should just walk away, especially if it was at work. I knew that no job paid well enough to allow someone to humiliate another person like that which is what I had done to the poor girl that morning. I was fully aware that the greatest humiliation was brought upon myself. Bob agreed and, like countless times before, expressed concern about my ability to handle stress.

That summer we visited England and my desire to die intensified. Throwing myself in front of a bus or big car was a recurring thought. At my lowest point it gave me pleasure to think that the end was near. Unfortunately drivers in England are very respectful of speed signs and drove too slowly to cause any serious damage to a careless pedestrian in all the areas where I was likely to be.

While we were in England, Bob did everything possible to ensure we all had a happy time. Nothing prepared the girls for a tantrum I threw early one morning as we were settling into the car to go out for the day. The girls were belted up in the back seat and Bob had the engine running and was ready to leave. I was walking quickly towards the car, carrying a coat.

'You don't need such a heavy coat. It will get warmer during the day. Why don't you find something lighter? There must be something in the suitcase,' said Bob as I got into the car. I immediately got out.

'Stop treating me like a child! I will wear a winter coat on a summer's day if I feel like it. Okay? An English summer is like winter to a tropical girl like me. If you're too embarrassed to see me bundled up like this, then go without me. Fuck you!' I said as I slammed the door shut.

He leaned over to open the door, looked at me angrily and ordered me to get in the car.

'No! No, no, no! I am not getting in! I'm not! If you make me, I will kill myself! I'm not going anywhere. I just want to die! Die, I want to die!' We were in a small village in the countryside. It was a quiet morning and my voice was louder than I thought possible. I saw someone peering through a curtain from the house down the driveway to see what was going on.

Bob looked over his shoulders to check on the girls. My eyes followed his. They were only thirteen years old. This was the first time they had seen me yell at Bob. Caroline was seated behind Bob, on the right side and was looking out the window. She was crying. Elena just glared at me. Within seconds of looking at them, I got in the car. We drove in silence for over an hour. The day was not as enjoyable as it should have been. I was racked with guilt and apologised. The girls were very forgiving and insisted they had a great time. That night as I lay in bed, I wondered if I might be losing my mind.

Thankfully, we did not have anything quite so dramatic for the rest of the holiday. I was too detached from Bob to make an effort to be a good wife.

When we returned from vacation I called my sister Rita who at that time was living in New Jersey. After a falling out that lasted over ten years during which we did not speak to each other, we had a patch-up during one of my visits to Toronto when she drove from upstate New York to see me. Since then, nearly five years earlier, I had made it a point to call her every few months. I told her about the two outbursts in a row in the past two weeks.

I wish I had told her about my various outbursts months, maybe years, before.

CHAPTER 7

'And something's odd – within –
That person that I was –
And this One – do not feel the same –
Could it be Madness – this?'
Emily Dickinson

My sister's voice was calm but I sensed she was reluctant to say something. Finally, she said something about inheriting Daddy's illness and that I should go and see a doctor. Wait, wait, wait ... what illness, what doctor?

'Daddy was *gila*. That's Malay for mad. Same thing, right? We never knew which way the wind was going to blow, remember? So unpredictable it was scary. He was too good to be true one day and the devil the next,' I said, remembering my father. 'I sometimes feel I'm losing it but I know I'm not. It's just stress. Advertising is a high-stress industry. Everybody goes through that,' I rambled, unsure I believed what I was saying.

'Daddy was manic-depressive and I think you might be, too. Think about what you just said about Daddy. Unpredictable, violent. Aren't you like that sometimes? It's hereditary. Not always but in most cases,' said Rita.

'Oh really? Manic-depressive. I think you've been in America for too long,' I said. 'When someone is a bit sad because the family dog died, the Americans call it depression and prescribe drugs. The rest of the world calls it grieving and recognises it as a natural process. When someone gets a little too angry, maybe too quickly, it is manic-depressive illness. The really crazy people are the ones who talk to themselves and the crazy evil ones are those who go on a rampage gunning down innocent people at the slightest provocation. I like America but I swear, too many people in that country are crazy and if you live there long enough, it will rub off on you. Even students and housewives have therapists. Oh for God's sake! I'm not crazy,' I was ranting, agitated and getting quite upset, at the same time wondering if there was some truth in what she just said.

'Oh please, Mahita! Why are you calling me? What do you want me to say? Don't worry, it's just stress? If you really believe it's stress, why call me to tell me all this? I was twelve when Amah thought your body was too heaty or you had bad spirits. We all believed it was your diet and possibly spirits, but do you believe that now? Seriously, do you?' she asked.

'I was fine after Mummy's special food, so maybe there was some truth there. Amah thought I was like Daddy but he was much worse. I'm not like Daddy. I'm not *gila*,' I said.

'Say what you want about America but we have the best scientists for mental illness research and probably the best hospitals. The manuals for diagnosis worldwide are published by leading American psychiatric organisations,' she said. 'Look, it's up to you but you've been like this since you became a stewardess. Maybe even before but it was more noticeable then. You can either see a doctor or ignore it and let this cycle repeat itself. Your choice. I'm only trying to help.'

She sounded impatient but at the same time like she was trying very hard not to sound sanctimonious.

'What about you? Maybe you have it too?' I suggested to my sister. Besides, she's no doctor, how would she know?

'Like I said, it's up to you. And by the way, one of my closest friends has been treated for depression for many years. That's when I learnt about mental disorders and their treatments. I have read extensively on the subject. What Daddy had is now called bipolar disorder. And yes, like many Americans, my friend sees a therapist. She finds those visits very helpful.' She sighed and said she had to go, it was getting late for her.

After she got off the phone, I thought about her words, whether there could be any truth in what she said. Was I really crazy like my father was? The kind of crazy that my mother sometimes said with a heavy sigh, a mixture of sadness and resignation in her voice, 'Castles in the sky, again'? My father was forever making plans to start some sort of business, like shipping sand from Indonesia for Singapore's booming construction industry. Or doing parallel imports of Johnny Walker Black Label Scotch because the Indian population was growing and not all Chinese people liked brandy. Or opening a restaurant serving home-style Kerala cuisine because there wasn't one in Singapore. The wildest plan he had was to convert to Islam so he could take a second wife to bear him a son. He had no plans to divorce my mother so he clearly had not realised that the first wife had to be Muslim too and give her consent to the second marriage and that the gender of a child was dependent on the father's chromosomes. He admired Hitler and cited *Mein Kampf* as his favourite book of all time. He was going to write a book based on the letters he would have written to Hitler as a teenager in Japanese-occupied Singapore. He did none of these things.

There were times when my mother slept on the floor in my older sister's room because my father had shut himself in the master bedroom, drawing the curtains close and sleeping for days on end. He was unkempt and often smelled. He was morose but at least he was calm, predictable and out of sight when he was like that. It was as if he could not summon the energy to scream at any of us. I did not feel sorry for him when he was in such a state. Instead, I was thankful for the peace and quiet.

When my father got into these moods, whether it was frightening eruptions or unfathomable melancholy, we usually stayed in our bedrooms. My mother would come to one of the two bedrooms shared between us three sisters and just sit on the floor. After a while she would quietly tell us that he needed help but we did not know what 'help' meant. Who would help him and what exactly would they do to help? After our older sister left home as soon as she turned twenty-one, Rita and I had been so repulsed by our father's behaviour that I think we had detached ourselves from him without realising it. I did not care whether or not anyone helped him and I certainly was not going to even try. My mother never said anything about mental illness or that help would have to come from a doctor.

One evening, my father came home, happy and smiling, with about six neckties from Dunhill, at the time regarded as the quintessential British gentleman's retailer. He said he had spent a few hundred dollars on them. My mother was outraged. I was speechless. He always favoured Swiss-made Bally shoes and tailored shirts but the purchase of these six expensive ties happened at a time when his real estate business was doing badly and my mother found it hard to cover our household expenses. I remembered with contempt how my father never had enough money to feed his family but always plenty for luxury shoes and clothes for himself.

I swore that one day I would kill him. I must have been around fourteen or fifteen years old at this time. Less than fifteen years later, I did. Sort of.

* * *

My older sister had come to visit me while I was pregnant. I had just turned twenty-nine barely two weeks before. She spoke of seeing our father regularly. I found it odd that she would bother to resume a relationship after the years of emotional, mental and physical abuse he heaped upon her since she was about three years old. I asked about his mistress who was my age and had seemed so lovely when I met her once by chance some years ago. I told my sister, in jest, that his mistress should just poison him slowly, let him die and run off with his money. About twelve hours later, around six in the morning, my sister called, crying hysterically.

'Daddy died. Heart attack. Ten minutes ago. He was fine. Fat but fine. Nothing wrong. There was nothing wrong. How can he just die without an illness?'

She was sobbing. I wondered if she was insinuating I had killed him because of what I had said. I was stunned into silence. By now Bob was sitting up asking what was wrong.

'How exactly did Daddy die?' I asked. Bob got his answer.

'Woke up to go to the bathroom, collapsed and died. First and last heart attack. Lucky, I suppose. But why did you have to say those things?'

There, she had said it. Somehow I had brought on his death. My older sister was crediting me with a power which I obviously did not have. We eventually agreed it was an eerie coincidence, nothing more.

I wept a little but I do not know why. It was not as if I was going to miss him so they were not tears of sorrow. I was relieved I did not have to introduce my twins, born just three weeks later, to a grandfather I rather they never knew.

* * *

My father alternated between being a very kind, obliging and generous person and a nasty hooligan on a rampage. He had many friends, people from various ethnic groups, people from all walks of life. He was often invited out for drinks and dinners at good restaurants. People liked him. They found him charming and agreeable and were naturally drawn to him. Most of his friends never saw his other side.

Rita's words kept playing in my head. Yes, my father was crazy but wasn't he schizo? Isn't that what all crazy people are – schizophrenic? Is manic-depressive just another type of schizo? Maybe the type where you don't hear voices? I knew nothing about mental illness other than what I had seen in the movies and they were almost always schizophrenic or pretended to be.

My weekend had just begun with me being told I might be crazy. I thought long and hard about this. I knew nothing and had to learn more. I was never more grateful for Google than on that very day when I could access important information privately.

Within an afternoon, I was able to put together a picture of me based on a juxtaposition of my memories and the words and phrases I read online.

* * *

Growing up, I was always very energetic and also a dreamer. I read a lot but had to re-read passages; during silent reading sessions in class, the teachers said I was easily distracted and didn't believe me when I said I wasn't dreaming but still I had to re-read passages over and over again. 'You're not slow so why are you taking so long?' they would say. 'Stop dreaming!' But I wasn't dreaming.

I asked a lot of questions in class. Sue got me started on that. Two or three teachers were glad for the questions because they knew other students wanted to know but were too shy or afraid to ask. Most just saw me as disruptive; they needed to teach a class of forty students and did not welcome any interruptions. Ms Lau, my favourite teacher was the only person who was forgiving and wrote in my report book that I was a most responsive student and a joy to teach.

I always felt a bit different in straight-laced Singapore; I was restless, jumpy, extroverted, extremely talkative and very imaginative especially when writing essays in school. Sometimes I was also irritable, listless, quiet and sad. The moods became more intense in my early twenties while I was at Singapore Airlines. Around the same time, the songs in my head played more often and more loudly. I had a repertoire of songs. Using the right song for a particular feeling comforted me. Queen was a perennial favourite: 'Under Pressure', 'I Want To Break Free' and 'Don't Stop Me Now'. I was sixteen when 'Don't Stop Me Now' was a huge hit and it just seemed to be my song. It spoke to me, about me. It became my mantra for years. It made me feel like a shooting star defying the laws of gravity, and sometimes like a racing car and other times burning through the sky, travelling at the speed of light … there was no stopping me.

There were weeks in a row when I was having such a good time I did not want to stop at all.

All the emotions – from restlessness to listlessness – along with the whole library of songs in my head came with an intensity which many people may have over the years secretly dismissed as craziness. Other than calling me names, usually *'Siao!'* or *'Sibeh siao*!' – Hokkien for crazy or very crazy respectively, and saying I was disruptive, nothing was done. My personality and behaviour were probably too overwhelming for the conservative, stifling environment in which I lived. Amah knew something was wrong but first believed it was Sue's American influence, and then later attributed it to a diet rich in spice and mutton which caused an imbalance in my whole being or spirits in my body.

I reviewed my early years, looking for answers. When I was

about eighteen, I was sitting at the dining table with my younger sister, waiting for our father to join us before we could start. He was washing his hands. He came and sat down at the head of the table holding the hand towel from the bathroom. Looking at my mother, and holding the towel, he screamed, 'This was on the bathroom floor!' My mother remained silent. 'I wash my hands only to put germs back from this filthy towel,' he boomed.

My mother sat on a chair across from the table, against the wall. I cannot remember why she was not at the table with us. Without warning, my father picked up his full glass of water and threw it at her. My sister and I watched in horror. It happened so quickly, and from where we sat there was no mistaking that he had aimed the glass at our mother's face. Fortunately he missed and the glass hit the wall right above my mother's head, shattering all around her. Except for a piece of glass that landed on her saree, everything was on the floor. The glass pieces only needed to be swept into a dustpan and thrown away. After more than twenty years' experience with such unpredictable explosions, even my mother was a little shocked by this particularly violent episode.

The evening when I told my father about the Police Protection Order remains the most frightening moment of my life. I walked into the lion's den, eyes wide open and faculties intact. My father could have killed me if had he been able to get out of his seat more quickly. Yet, I did not seem to think about the consequences, focusing solely on the objective of getting him out of the house.

Looking back at those events that were still so vivid in my memory, I wondered about my own fits of temper. Were they all out of proportion in relation to the situation? Bob had used the words 'out of proportion' several times over the years, long before I would see the relevance when reading about bipolar disorder. My mind replayed events from years before. I didn't have to scream like a banshee and curse the poor kid at the supermarket for forgetting to defrost the turkey; we could have had chicken or ham for Christmas and roast the turkey another day. It was totally out of proportion. There was no need to scream at our helper just because she forgot the tomatoes in the soup; she should not have lied but it was still good soup. There was no need to wish death upon that motorcyclist; his stupidity and recklessness would probably kill him anyway; my screaming upset the kids; I needed to focus on the driving; this was out of proportion; that was out of proportion. Over a period of nearly fifteen years, 'out of proportion' was an oft-heard phrase and one I eventually learnt to tune out.

The screaming at the designer and calling him a small man, the threat to kill myself that quiet morning in England and shouting at the executive in my office asking if she was retarded were all certainly out of proportion. There had been a number of others, but were they as intense or as violent? I could not be the judge of that, no matter how objective I tried to be.

* * *

I thought about the time I came home from work, in a good mood, and found Bob and the girls in the nursery. With their bucket of Lego pieces, they had created a large area of green for land and blue for sea. They had made houses for the land mass and little boats for the sea. As soon as they saw me, they said 'Look Mummy, look what we made', their faces beaming and smiling brightly.

'What the fuck do you think you're doing? This is a monumental mess! Clear it up! NOW!' I screamed as I kicked the pieces on the floor and the land and sea were now just a big mess, pieces spread all over the room. My face was contorted and my eyes were wild like someone possessed. That was my response – unexpected, uncalled for, and plain nasty. The girls were horrified. I do not know what made me respond in such a manner. That night Bob said to me that I had overreacted and what I said was hurtful to the girls. Only then did I feel some remorse but not enough to feel that something was wrong. Bob put it down to stress at work. He was convinced I was fundamentally incapable of self-control.

* * *

Tempers flare all the time. People say hurtful things, sometimes also really stupid things. They overreact, some get violent. Almost always the reactions are unwarranted but such reactions do not mean they are crazy. Or do they?

I thought about all those times when I amazed myself by what I thought to be exceptional generosity and spontaneity. The generosity was usually limited to shopping for the children. Six sets of cotton pyjamas when they already had four perfectly good sets each and were still growing. Coloured gel pens with sparkles which they did not need because they already had so many. More buckets of Lego. It was wasteful at a time when we could not afford to be, but the girls did not know this and like most children, they were happy to be given more. What fun they had when they thought they were just two minutes from home, the Sunday afternoon outing about to come to an end, when I would drive past the entrance to our home, turn the music way up, wind the windows down, and hit the highway while we played Don McLean's 'American Pie'. I smiled to myself as I looked into the rear view mirror and saw the looks of delight shining on their faces as they sang along. They sang bye bye to Miss American Pie, they believed in rock and roll, they sang about the court jester, birds falling fast, nimble Jack and heading for the coast They were nine years old and knew all the words. It was priceless.

When was it a sense of fun and spontaneity and when did it become mania?

There were moments of spontaneity with my father, except

it was almost exclusively related to food. My father adored Singapore street food, something which I inherited and have over the past ten years turned into an obsession. Just as we had cleaned our teeth and said goodnight, he would suggest a thirty-minute drive to Changi Beach for *ice kacang*, a delightful concoction of sweet red beans covered with a pyramid of shaved ice drizzled with thick syrup in garish shades of red, green and orange. Another night it would be satay, and I would dream of the tender pieces of marinated beef, grilled to perfection over hot coals, and that chunky peanut sauce for dipping as we drove to the Satay Club at the Esplanade and return home at about midnight, on a school night. During these times, my father was generous and great fun. We could not see anything crazy about someone like that, even if everything was exaggerated. My older sister and I always jumped at the chance. My mother always stayed at home with my younger sister who would usually be long asleep. Once Amah had left, my parents did not encourage the bedtime routine Amah had lovingly and patiently established. We were pretty much left to our own devices in a home headed by a very moody and unpredictable father who could be so much fun one moment and a terrifying bully the next. The situation was exacerbated by a mother who escaped to a world of Hindu fellowship chanting devotional hymns with a few friends who were devout followers of some Guru or another.

* * *

It was Sunday night, late July 2005. By the time I went to bed, I decided to contact a psychiatrist the next morning for an earliest possible appointment. It was more to rule out mental illness than to confirm it. I had a husband many women could only dream about, the kind who ensures a life of security and comfort for his family. I had two beautiful children who were well-adjusted and well-behaved; friends and acquaintances have been known to single them out when talking about wonderful teenagers. I had the most amazing circle of friends – I loved their company and knew I could always count on them. Almost every job I had and every brand I had worked on had been with a company ranked number one or very highly on any given Forbes' or Fortune list. I was very good at what I did.

Mentally ill people just aren't that blessed. Maybe there is some truth to the saying 'The Good Lord giveth and the Good Lord taketh' but I could not believe that when the Good Lord took away my sanity, He blessed with a wonderful family, strong friendships with incredible people and a satisfying career. So, I had to rule out mental illness.

I wanted to prove my sister wrong. I did not have bipolar disorder or any kind of mental illness and I was not like my father. On Tuesday afternoon, I saw Professor Sim, one of Singapore's top psychiatrists in private practice. He was one of two recommended by our family doctor. I postponed a client meeting and went to see Professor Sim. I was assured by his kindly demeanour and his grey hair which suggested a very experienced doctor.

He asked me many questions, most of them very personal. He stressed that answers had to be honest and qualified with examples. Even though I was familiar with many of the questions having read them on various websites, I was not prepared for my reaction. I found some of them too personal and intrusive. Do you often feel extremely energetic? Do you have a very active sex life? Have you been promiscuous? Are you an impulsive person? Are you involved in a goal-directed activity? How many hours of sleep do you need? Tell me about the last time you lost your temper and what caused it. Are you very talkative, speaking very quickly? What about times when you've been very sad, have you experienced that before? Do people have trouble keeping up with you? How much caffeine do you consume a day? Do you crave sugar or sweet things like cake and ice cream? Do you shop impulsively, buying things you do not need or many quantities of the same items? Tell me your plans for the future. Do you have a family history of mental illness? Alcohol or substance abuse? Suicide attempts or thoughts of suicide?

'Doctor, I have answered all your questions honestly and I can see from that clipboard in front of you that there are a lot more. I don't see how all this is any of your business. My sex life and future plans are personal,' I said and before he could respond,

I continued 'Why would you care how much Diet Coke I drink every day or how talkative I am?

'Unlike most major illnesses, mental disorders are not diagnosed using blood tests and brain scans. I have to ask you all these questions. They are part of a set of criteria from *The Diagnostic and Statistical Manual for Mental Disorders*. We evaluate your symptoms before making a diagnosis. Don't worry, it is very reliable and is widely respected and used worldwide. As it is by the American Psychiatric Association it is also thorough and very professional,' said Professor Sim.

'Diagnosis? Does that mean you decided I was *siao* as soon as I sat down, before asking the questions? I'm not here to confirm mental illness okay? I'm here to rule it out! To prove my American sister wrong. I'm sure she has a lot of faith in your manual but she's wrong,' I said. Sitting in his office, I wanted to be anything but mad.

'Ms Mahita, I understand how you feel. I see first-time patients regularly. An evaluation is the first step. Let's continue.'

After ninety minutes of questioning and talking, he told me I had experienced a full manic episode over the past week and had several episodes in the past. He said that the current symptoms had been going on for long enough to prevent me from functioning normally. We discussed my previous history of mania and depression before he pronounced me bipolar and started to tell me about the medication he was going to prescribe. Stunned by all this information, I asked how it was possible to diagnose a serious illness, one that requires lifelong medication and carries a stigma, with nothing more than a question and answer session.

'There isn't a definitive test. It is not unusual for younger people, those in their teens and early twenties, to be wrongly diagnosed which could be worse than not being diagnosed at all. I am basing my diagnosis on the criteria we discussed earlier and on my decades of experience as a doctor,' he said.

As I continued to sit in the doctor's office, allowing the diagnosis to sink in, I recalled seeing what he had just told me on virtually every medical website during my research over the weekend. Clear as it seemed, I simply could not come to terms with how the doctor could possibly give me a definitive diagnosis and put me on medication. I was aware about a long list of symptoms for manic-depressive illness. I knew that not every symptom needed to be present for a diagnosis. However, all the symptoms could just as easily be associated with any random person.

'Maybe I'm just an extreme person. Not psycho. Like in the Billy Joel song about going to extremes. I know all the words. Sometimes I'm this and sometimes I'm that. Just like everyone I know, probably like you, too. Only thing is I'm a lot more expressive and it's more noticeable here because the Chinese aren't very expressive. Doesn't make me mental,' I said.

'Yes, maybe you are just an extreme person. With bipolar disorder, you establish a pattern of extreme behaviour as evidenced by the presence and duration of your signs and symptoms. That is one of the biggest tell-tale signs, the pattern of your mood swings from mania to depression. Medication and therapy will help you be more balanced. I will prescribe some medication which you should take diligently. I will see you next week for a follow up,' said Professor Sim.

Medication and therapy? By now, I was very upset.

'Don't most people at some point have mood swings, happy today and sad tomorrow or even the same day? Don't many people shop impulsively? Surely it isn't the bipolar world keeping retail alive? Unless you're rich and famous, who does not dream about a life other than the one you have now? Don't a lot of people get by on too little sleep? Don't most people do this? Doesn't everyone do that?' I asked, raising my voice.

He could tell that I was having much trouble accepting the diagnosis. We had lost track of my questions. He went on to explain the medication and the importance of taking them in the right dosage at the right time.

I asked Professor Sim how he could be so sure and how he could think it was all right to medicate me based on a ninety-minute meeting. Professor Sim explained that my mood swings were intense and followed a pattern defined as episodes. A normal person loses his temper but I have an episode; my flare ups follow a pattern. Patterns and episodes, words that determined my sorry mental state to an absolute certainty.

'What about all those people with terrible tempers? Famous actors who attack photographers, for instance?' I asked, still hoping he may have made a mistake. Besides, Sean Penn was my number one favourite actor and notoriously temperamental but had not been portrayed by the media as bipolar; he was ideal for comparison.

'I cannot comment on people like that. Also, it's not just about a quick temper. That is just one-dimension. Bipolar is multi-dimensional. There are the mood swings, going from increased self-esteem to feeling worthless, from being excessively happy to intensely sad. That is just the most basic level of what a mood swing is and the pattern you've displayed so far.' I was not sure if his reply was helpful.

Other people may shop impulsively but I am having an episode when I spend $1,000 buying ten bottles of Clarins anti-cellulite lotion for my slim and relatively toned thirty-five-year-old body, never having used such lotions before and probably was never going to.

I just did not understand what he was saying. It was not sinking in. Bipolar disorder sounded a lot more sinister than manic-depressive illness. He told me it was the same thing – the Americans had renamed it in 1980. Ah yes, the Americans. I told him I once wanted to be American. The same people who call the blind 'visually impaired' and garbage collectors 'sanitation engineers'.

'Do you think the term bipolar disorder makes it easier for a person to accept a diagnosis of mental illness at best and insanity at worst? That even with medication the sufferer will probably experience manic and depressive episodes for the rest of his or her life?' I asked.

'For some, no it does not make a difference. For others, bipolar disorder sounds less like a mental illness so they feel better. It becomes a problem when they do not take the diagnosis seriously and skip their medication,' he said.

Bipolar disorder. Manic-depressive. Manic episode. Depressive episode. Triggers. Psychosis. Mania. Full-blown. Anticonvulsants.

It was all just too much for me. Too much, too soon.

I got up, left the room and waited for the medication to be packed and explained. I then paid the biggest bill I had ever incurred for consultation and medication on a visit to the doctor. I went to the office and checked my emails. It was nearly the end of the day and seeing that there was nothing urgent on my desk, I packed up and went home.

That night, I started on my medication. After a day off, Bob was leaving for another short trip the next morning. I decided not to alarm him so he could go on his flight blissfully unaware that he was married to an insane woman. Not wanting another manic episode, I diligently took the medication for three days. I cannot remember what the doctor gave me but there were three kinds of pills and I remember the words 'anti-psychotic' and 'sedative'.

I did not go to work for two days. I slept most of the time. I was too sluggish to take calls from my team or from clients. I stopped the medication on the third day because I felt numb, like I was soon going to be a vegetable. It was another few days before I felt I was getting closer to my old self again, although not quite. I decided not to tell anyone about the visit to the doctor. I threw away the anti-psychotic pills but I don't know why I felt the need to keep the sleeping pills. I cancelled my next appointment which was due that Friday.

* * *

Several months went by peacefully, or so I thought. I was looking forward to ending the year without another manic or depressive episode. No more doctors, no more medication. That seemed too much to ask for.

One afternoon, after a few weeks of working late, all I wanted to do was to go home early and be with my children. However, I had to meet my boss, Sorab, for drinks that evening, pre-arranged earlier that week. It was my first time going out for a drink after work with a boss and I felt uncomfortable but another colleague assured me that Sorab was being thoughtful and that he felt in some instances it was better to say things about work in a non-corporate environment.

I met Sorab at Blu Bar in Shangri-La hotel just before seven that evening. He ordered red wine and I had a club soda.

'So, how are things going for you?' Sorab asked.

'Everything's fine, Sorab. Thank you for asking.'

He nodded slowly and then turned to look at me. In those few seconds before he spoke, I knew he was going to say something that would upset me.

'People in the office are talking about your exuberance,' he turned to look at his drink.

I was stunned by his tone. What did he mean by 'people are talking' and who were they? I was not even aware that I was exuberant. How did my exuberance bother them and how bad could it be? He could tell I was gathering my thoughts. I had not noticed manic symptoms recently, unlike during the Air Force pitch which was months ago. Clearly others had.

In the early days of my diagnosis just months before, I read extensively to make sense of an illness about which I knew very little. One of the books was *Exuberance: The Passion For Life* by Dr Kay Redfield Jamison. It struck a chord with its study of this effervescent emotion and offered examples ranging from John Muir to Franklin Roosevelt to Mary Poppins and Peter Pan. Not knowing what my colleagues had said and what other behaviours might bother them in the near future, I decided to come clean.

'I'm unwell,' I said, looking straight at him. 'I have bipolar disorder. Type 1, the most severe form. I found out a couple of months ago. Took medication for a few days and stopped.

Exuberance is common during a manic high.'

Sorab did not look surprised. He stared into his drink. I wondered if he might have had some idea of the illness but may not have met someone afflicted with it. Sensing I might be a problem to him and his team, I decided I needed to do something.

'I'll see a doctor in the next few days. I'll get a second opinion and if I really have bipolar disorder, I'll stick to my medication. I know medication can keep things under control and help me live a normal life. Really, Sorab. Please let me sort this out.' Taking my medication was a promise I knew I had to keep.

Through my family doctor, I managed to get an emergency appointment with the other psychiatrist he had recommended previously – Dr Soh, a highly regarded psychiatrist in private practice. I saw him at seven-thirty the next morning. He explained that it was necessary to go through the evaluation process again as I did not have my medical files with me. The questions were phrased differently but my answers were the same.

'So I am really sick then? And there is no cure? Definitely bipolar disorder? Type 1?' I asked Dr Soh.

'Yes. You have an incurable illness but with medication and therapy you can function like any normal person. I am prescribing mood stabilisers as well as anti-psychotics and anti-depressants,' said Dr Soh.

'But how? How did I get this illness? What causes bipolar disorder?' I already knew the answers from my earlier visit to

Professor Sim and through my research on the Internet but was hoping to hear something different.

'No one knows for sure. There isn't one particular cause but some people are genetically predisposed to bipolar disorder. Like you. Doesn't mean those with an inherited vulnerability develop the illness, which suggests why your sisters don't have it. Some research shows neurotransmitter imbalances, abnormal thyroid function and high levels of the stress hormone cortisol can also cause bipolar disorder. This means anyone can get it. No one knows what causes bipolar disorder and no one is immune.'

It sounded too scientific for me but I understood enough to know Dr Soh had just confirmed my worst fears I was mentally ill and there was no cure.

'Does this mean I have to be on medication for the rest of my life? And will medication mean I will never scream at my children or anyone again? That I will not feel like wanting to die? That I won't take to my bed and cry for nothing?' I asked, still trying to make sense of the diagnosis.

'I cannot promise that. External factors like a situation or event can bring on an episode. These are called triggers and directly affect mood stability. Medication will help stabilise your moods but episodes and symptoms depend on the triggers. Therapy can help you monitor your mood swings and manage your triggers so you can reduce your symptoms. It will take time but you must stay on your medication and commit to therapy,' he said.

'I don't want another episode. I will take my medication and go for therapy,' I said, with every intention of taking control of my illness.

'Just so you know, some patients do experience manic rages and depression even on medication. It is still possible to find yourself in a situation, despite years of medication, reacting like a bipolar patient who was never treated. Just be aware. This is why staying on your medication is critical. It drastically lowers the risk of this happening.'

'So you are saying that I can take my medication yet suffer a manic or depressive episode? How?'

'There are still many things science cannot explain about mental illness. It is critical that you maintain your dosage. As long as you are disciplined about your medication, it is unlikely you will experience a relapse. Don't worry, you'll feel better in no time.' Dr Soh had a reassuring manner. 'You know, I have been to court a few times as an expert witness, usually for the defence. You'll be surprised what trouble people can get into during a manic rage. The courts are aware of the effects of various mental disorders including bipolar disorder and schizophrenia and when presented as a mitigating factor, a convicted, mentally ill criminal may be committed to long-term psychiatric care instead of prison.'

I left Dr Soh's office with several types of medication. Memories of incidents in Rome, Paris and various other places came flooding back. I did not want to go to jail or be confined to a mental hospital. I promised myself I would take them diligently, carrying spares in my bag in case I forgot a dose at home. I was full of hope.

* * *

People were talking about me at the office, according to Sorab. I wanted them to stop. I was now determined to take all the help that was available and start living like all my normal friends and family.

I immediately started on Lamotrigine twice a day to stabilise my moods and therapy every few days and quickly started to feel better. A few nights later after dinner, I told Bob about my visit to the doctor. I did not tell him my visit was triggered by what Sorab had said.

'Your wife is mentally ill. My screaming and shouting became too much even for me so I saw a doctor. Actually, I saw one when we returned from Europe but I threw away the pills after a few days. This time I went to see another doctor for a second opinion,' I said. I noticed he was silent and listened carefully as I spoke. 'I have bipolar disorder. The Americans coined this term for manic-depressive illness. There's no cure, just lifelong medication and a healthy lifestyle. I'm in good company, though. According to the Internet, I now have something in common with Churchill, Lincoln, Mozart, Virginia Woolf, Hemingway and Kurt Cobain. Oh and Nietzsche too. There is hope yet, Bob. I don't think I'm ready to compose an opus or be President yet, though.'

There was a long silence. He was processing the information, which was a lot to take in, coming so unexpectedly.

'It makes sense, doesn't it? Your behaviour was too extreme to be normal. I just thought it was your strong personality and lack of self-control. I suppose it's good that you have identified the problem and there's a solution. Have you read books about this illness? We should learn more about it. Research it for the right treatment,' he said, relieved that my abominable behaviour in the past was caused by a chemical imbalance and not an innate wickedness or lack of will over myself. There was now an explanation and a name for the extreme behaviour he had witnessed over the past two decades. We told the children that weekend.

'You know how Mummy would scream at you sometimes, especially when you were little? Say bad things that made you cry? When Caroline asked me to please stop but I just could not and went on and on?' I asked and noticed Caroline, my more sensitive child, was already tearing. It broke my heart to realise that not only did she remember, but also how my screams affected her. They both nodded. 'Well, I have some good news. All that screaming should stop now. I went to see a doctor who said that I am not well. There are some chemicals in my brain that are basically out of whack. It affects how I feel and how I behave, how I respond to people and situations. Like the time a several months ago when I screamed at the dentist and his patient for making us wait for half an hour. Remember that? Just because the patient jumped the queue and the dentist allowed it was no reason scream at both of them, right?'

'So what sickness do you have, Mummy? Is it brain cancer? Will you be okay?' asked Elena.

'No, not cancer! I have bipolar disorder. It is an illness that can be treated with medication. It is not something to be ashamed of but at the same time not something to announce to your friends, either. I am going to be fine and will start being a much calmer person from now on,' I said, with every intention of sticking to my medication. 'I am very, very sorry for all the screaming and the bad things I have said to you in the past. Also for throwing away all those things you kept in your drawers because I could not stand the mess in your room. You no longer have to squirm or cry because I will not be screaming like a mad woman anymore.'

Soon after I got on Lamotrigine, I lost weight rapidly. I went from my average forty-five kilograms down to forty-one in six weeks despite maintaining my appetite. Rather than try to put on weight, I went out and got a whole new wardrobe of size zero clothes which still needed to be taken in. I felt good about being size less-than-zero for the first time since I was a stewardess. At the same time, I knew this was not a healthy weight and started eating more, mainly all the wrong foods. It didn't help that my office was on Orchard Road. After weeks on end of Häagen-

Dazs milkshakes, chocolate éclairs, cream puffs and other cakes, chocolate and ice cream, my weight inched up by a kilogram. I did not think it was a problem. I was the envy of everyone I knew – unrestrained gorging without having to worry about weight gain.

Work was not as stimulating as it used to be. During the first six weeks, I also had to take some other medication along with Lamotrigine. I was given Venlafaxine for depression and Aripiprazole as an anti-psychotic for the mania. I found it extremely hard to cope with the side effects and several times considered throwing them all away. On any given day, depending on what medication I was on, I felt at least two of the following: sleepiness, nausea, dry mouth, chills, weakness, restlessness and dizziness. I also had nightmares, stomach cramps, and my head hurt. Clumsiness and weakness in my limbs was the most noticeable and distressful side effect especially during lunch at a food court, when I had to carry a tray with a bowl of boiling hot noodle soup and a drink. I also felt weepy, got tired easily and had to suck on mints constantly just to take away the dryness in my mouth. The doctor assured me these were common side effects and advised me to give it time.

On top of that, I was still trying to come to terms with the fact that I was mentally ill. I was ashamed and afraid. I did not want to keep taking the medication and wondered if I would have to stay in a mental hospital at some point. I was afraid to lose what mattered to me most in the whole world – my children, Bob and a small circle of friends.

Whether due to the side effects of the medication or my erratic consumption resulting in messing up my head even more, I became increasingly despondent by the day. Now, more than ever, I wanted to die.

I was too subdued and missed my old self. In those days, even at my worst, when I was listless, I knew I would bounce back in no time. Right now, I did not know if this was the new me. It was taking too long to feel better, to feel 'normal'. I could not and did not want to wait.

CHAPTER 8

'I thought how unpleasant it is to be locked out; and I thought how it is worse, perhaps, to be locked in.'

Virginia Woolf

In the first week of November, the urge to die weaved its way in and out of my head with frightening regularity and depth. I did not want to talk to Dr Soh because by now I had read a few memoirs and several books written by experts all of which said that such thoughts meant having to spend time in a mental hospital or go for electroconvulsive treatment, either of which would have been essential in helping me get over my suicidal thoughts. I was determined not to go to hospital; it was all too reminiscent of *One Flew Over the Cuckoo's Nest*, which I watched just a month earlier as a misjudged attempt at education.

Around mid-November 2005, after a slow Friday morning, I met Bina, one of my closest friends for lunch which we planned the week before. It was a leisurely lunch, most pleasurable, and I tried not to show what was really going through my head. She sensed something was wrong and asked me. She did not push me, preferring to trust me instead, when I said I was fine. I then went back to work and finished whatever I could for the day. I left the office at five o'clock and drove to Singapore Polo Club where the children were having their riding lessons. They were due to start at five-fifteen and end at six in the evening. I was going to watch them. I was sure it would lift my spirits and the bad thoughts in my head would go away. The children were surprised and happy to see me. We went home and had a special dinner. I opened a bottle of Moet et Chandon champagne and poured it into three exquisite champagne glasses. Bob collected champagne glasses and we had about twelve different ones. I let them choose their glass.

'What are we celebrating, Mummy?' asked Caroline as she held a beautiful handmade Lalique glass with just enough champagne for two or three sips.

'Life,' I said. 'We are celebrating life.'

'What is it about life that we are celebrating?' asked Elena. I was not expecting a question like that and did not know how to answer it. 'Just life,' I said smiling at them, thinking how lovely they were. I picked up my glass to toast and they obediently did the same. By eight thirty, they were in bed, exhausted from a full week of school and activities and a little light-headed from the champagne. Bob was coming home at around eleven-thirty that night from Beijing, and Caroline was leaving for Chiang Mai on a two-week school trip on Saturday afternoon for which we were all going to help her pack.

Soon after they went to bed, I wrote a few very personal words on pretty cards for Elena, Caroline and Bob. I told them I adored them but bad things were happening inside my head and I did not know what else to do or where else to go. I begged them to forgive me. I had loads of stationery, buying them the way I did cellulite lotion. Stocking up without the need for them. This time though, having some cards lying around came in handy.

After writing the cards to the three most important people in my life, I thought about things I wanted to say to a few friends. I wrote a few more cards. Then I thought about other people – colleagues, former colleagues, people who had made a difference in my life, people to whom I had not been particularly kind. The list was rapidly growing in my mind. That's when I thought to send an email. I did not have much time. I then started on an email. I just wrote as it came to my head. I was not sure why I was writing it and to whom I was going to send it. It was the most difficult note I had ever written but I remember it did not take long to write. When I finished it I sent it to nearly everyone on my email address book, without hesitation. I meant to send it to others as well, mainly former colleagues at Four Seasons, but they were not on my Yahoo mail address book.

Here is what I wrote:

Friends,

Please forgive me for this broadcast email. I have made a sudden decision to go away and will not be contactable for a long time so PLEASE DO NOT WRITE BACK AND PLEASE DO NOT CALL!!!

What I'm about to tell you may come as a surprise to most of you but may not be such a surprise to some of you, especially those with whom I worked very closely over a long period.

In the middle of the year, I was depressed and during a visit to one of the city's top psychiatrists, I was diagnosed as being manic-depressive and was treated for the condition with supplementary treatment for depression. But at the time I did not quite understand what it was all about and when the medications made me feel dopey, I quit after three or four days and didn't go back to the doctor. Things didn't get that much better but I managed somehow.

Then after some incidents in early October, I saw the same doctor again and learned more about manic-depressive illness, also politely known as bipolar disorder. I got a second opinion from another leading psychiatrist the next day and was given the same diagnosis.

I was then put on long-term treatment combined with short-term medication for depression/anxiety, and some psychotherapy/counselling.

As you can imagine, it was very difficult to accept the news of this illness. It doesn't appear to be a big deal in North America where celebrities are poster boys and girls for bipolar disorder, but it is very different here. It is something that is not expected to be shared with just anybody.

For years before the diagnosis, there were many days when it was a struggle for me to feel happy or interested, and looking back now, to just feel 'normal'. There were days of profound sadness and scary days of manic overdrive when uncontrollable rage was the order of the day. But of course there were some amazing highs too! It never ever crossed my mind that any of it was abnormal, but looking back, I can see it all very clearly now. A lot was simply not normal by any definition.

I think the only reason I did relatively well in my career was because the advertising industry is a perfect camouflage for psychosis. It's almost as if such behaviour is condoned, if not encouraged. I guess ad types see it as passion or infectious exuberance or whatever. In any case, I think it's only gotten worse in the past eight to ten years, during which time I always gave my best and delivered the work.

Since the diagnosis, I have been riddled with overwhelming shame and guilt from looking back at all those things that were said and done to various people – family, strangers, friends and colleagues. My family and closest friends keep telling me to look forward and not back but as much as I try, it's difficult to do. I think this quote clearly expresses what I'm going through:

'*Yet it is in our idleness, in our dreams, that the submerged truth sometimes comes to the top.*'
Virginia Woolf (also known to have been manic-depressive)

But the truths are very hard to face, the truths are the reasons for the immense guilt and shame. I have tried to kill those demons but I feel that every time I slay a demon, two others pop up. I feel the only way out is to run away from them. I know it's a cowardly thing to do but my only goal is to find peace inside and this is my only option.

I just wanted to thank you for your friendship all these years, for all your support and kindness. For those of you who were unfortunate enough to experience one of my manic rages, I can only apologise. For those of you, which is most of you, if not ALL of you, who in one way or another added to my life's good experiences, I thank you :)

Good bye. God bless you.

Kind regards, Mahita

With just one press of a button, nearly one hundred and fifty people all over the world received this email.

It was now nine-thirty at night. I switched off the computer before any responses came in and called my mother who was living in Los Angeles. She was not on the email list. I told her I was not well and she said she would pray for me. We spoke for fifteen minutes about her health and her friends. When the call ended, I left the phone off the hook.

I went to the kitchen, took the bottle of leftover champagne, the little packet of sleeping pills I got from Professor Sim in August, a stiff and waxy plastic carrier bag from Marks and Spencer, a roll of thick packing tape and a box cutter. I went to the guest room and shut the door. The lock didn't work so I pushed a table against the door. I drank a glass of champagne and looked at the time. It was just before ten o'clock at night. Bob was expected back in about ninety minutes, which gave me more than enough time to get prepared for a sound sleep and not make a mess. I did not, could not, think about anything else.

I had another glass of champagne and took eight pills, all that was left from the ten I had been given previously. I finished the second glass of champagne and slid the carrier bag over my head. I specifically chose the Marks & Spencer one because it was the perfect size and being made from a stiff and waxy plastic, it would be impossible for me to tear it off with my stubby fingers if I panicked and changed my mind at the last minute. This important detail only occurred to me when I was rummaging in the store room for an appropriate bag. I then ran the packing tape – soft plastic which was easy to twirl around and wide enough to cover large areas – across my face and under my chin and ensured every bit was tightly sealed. Before I could finish, I could feel the deepest sleep about to swallow me. As I cut the tape, I thought about also slashing my wrists, just to be sure, but it seemed too violent and would have been messy. I was also afraid of the pain from a deep gash. I put the cutter away and lay down to sleep on the floor. I instinctively looked at my watch but could not see through the translucent bag. I could not tell how many minutes had passed. I knew that I would be asleep in seconds and suffocate in fifteen minutes, thirty tops, with the life sucked completely out of me long before Bob got home.

I felt happy and calm and completely at peace. A moment later, I felt nothing. I must have fallen asleep and as far as I knew just before then, I was not going to wake up again. For decades I had thought of death, my own death on my own terms.

Now, Death and I were finally going to meet. I was looking forward to seeing Amah.

CHAPTER 9

'To run away from trouble is a form of cowardice and,
while it is true that the suicide braves death, he does it not
for some noble object but to escape some ill.'

Aristotle

I remember the scent of Dove shower cream and then stirring
before slowly opening my eyes. The harsh glare of the ceiling
lights startled me and then I saw Bob's face. A sad, ashen face
looking at me, quite bewildered. I was in the hospital, on a gurney,
waiting to be admitted. My housekeeper Ani was sponging me.
Why would she be doing that?

'It didn't work,' I muttered feebly as the reality of my suicide
attempt slowly dawned on me. I was trying to piece together in
my drug-hazed mind how my water-tight plan could possibly
have gone wrong.

'Shhhh,' said Bob gently, with a hand held out flat near my
face, a signal to be quiet.

He leaned over me and whispered. 'They are going to ask
you questions. You took some pills in a moment of foolishness

and swallowed them with champagne,' he said and waited for my response.

My mind was blank. I was offended by the phrase 'moment of foolishness'. I thought it was a clever plan. He was still looking at me.

'Do you understand me? Nod if you do.'

I nodded, just as a nurse wheeled me in to see a doctor. Emotions ranging from disappointment to fear to anger to self-pity were welling up inside me all at once. Even in that moment of turmoil in my head, I immediately sensed the doctor's hostility. His whole manner, his tone, even the look on his face made me see him as an enemy. My defences were up and I was suddenly, miraculously, more lucid.

'Did you try to kill yourself?' he asked.

'No. Why would I do that?' I asked in return, staring at the ceiling. I remember thinking my response was flat and unconvincing. Maybe it sounded too defensive.

'So why did you swallow so many pills? With alcohol on top of that?' The tone was decidedly accusing and condescending. He walked towards where I was lying and looked at me.

'I didn't think they were that many. I've taken three in the past, when I had a lot of trouble sleeping,' I lied. 'I didn't think eight was that many. I was desperate to get some sleep.'

'The alcohol?' he asked, writing on his clipboard.

'Champagne isn't really alcohol is it? I mean our kids were

given champagne when they were four,' I answered and caught myself a little too late.

'Of course it is alcohol. Children should not be drinking it,' he responded curtly. I wanted to tell him that my children do, only when celebrating and only a little but it still goes down their little throats and into their little bellies.

'Oh. Well it just seemed like a nice idea. I figured it would make the pills more effective. I just wanted to sleep for fifteen hours. I was not trying to kill myself,' I said, not sure if he was convinced. I was suddenly aware of the consequences and was afraid he was going to call the police. Or maybe he was not going to call the police because he was a kind doctor who personally thought the law governing attempted suicide was archaic and unfair to people like me.

He said I would need to be admitted for at least a day for observation. As I was wheeled out, I saw a large white clock, with spiky but elegant black hands telling me it was one-thirty in the morning.

I had gone to sleep nearly four hours ago. I was not supposed to wake up ever again. What had happened? What had gone wrong? How? Why?

I heard the nurse asking Bob if he wanted to go to the hospital room with me. The nurse left soon after wheeling me into the room and showing me where the call button was. Bob helped me undress and get into the hospital bed. As I lay down, trying to find a comfortable position, I saw Bob sitting at the edge of the bed, looking out the large windows. The surrounding buildings had all their public areas lit, casting a pretty orange-yellow glow. In more than twenty years together, I had never witnessed such a look on his face. The combination of dejection, sadness, fear and mostly incredulity made him look so vulnerable. Bob had always been my pillar of strength, my anchor, my giant and watching him sitting there in silence was more than I could bear. It cut me to the bone.

'What happened?' I asked, summoning the courage and breaking the unbearable silence.

'You tell me,' he replied. His voice was soft, with a hint of resignation.

'I wanted to die. It was a fool-proof plan. What happened?' I asked again.

He looked at me. I noticed how much he had aged since he had left for Beijing two days before. His eyes were soft and gentle, as I had always known them to be. He wasn't angry, he wasn't judging me. He just wanted to understand.

'You often said you feel blessed. Amongst your many blessings, you counted me for being a loyal and reliable husband who takes good care of his family. You ask the girls to give thanks for me, their daddy, for the same reasons. You always said you were thankful for having good kids, good friends and a good job,' he said. I was surprised he remembered my conversation about my thanksgiving prayers. 'If you count all these as your blessings, then why would you want to die? I don't understand'.

'I don't know. I cannot explain it. I have thought many times about dying. For years and years the thoughts would come and go. I remember telling you about it, a long time ago and you said "Everyone thinks of death at some point". So I thought it was normal. This just seemed a good time. I hate what's going on inside my head. Please tell me what happened, Bob. Please. What went wrong?' I begged him to tell me.

'You spoke about death in general. Not suicide. That is not normal. Anyway, you wanted to know what happened. I came home nearly an hour earlier,' he started to explain but I interrupted him.

'What? How is that even possible to be an hour early on a seven-hour flight?' I asked, realising I had not even thought to allow for an early arrival. He had never ever been home more than thirty minutes early, certainly not since we moved much further away from the airport fifteen years before. Unlike most pilots who favoured the East Coast area for the proximity to Changi Airport, we chose to live in Bukit Timah which was quite a distance from the airport.

'We had strong tailwinds, not unusual for this time of the year. That took nearly thirty minutes off the flying time. I didn't have a trainee, which was very unusual. He called in sick before we left Singapore. That saved at least ten, maybe even fifteen, minutes from the debriefing and filing a report,' he answered. He spoke softly, matter-of-factly, looking straight into my eyes.

He paused, as if carefully thinking about his next words.

'The real time saver was the taxi,' he continued. 'Scheduled arrival was 10.35 pm but we landed at 10.10 pm so we didn't get crew taxi. I usually end up waiting a good twenty minutes for a crew taxi so sometimes I just don't bother and I head for the taxi rank. Tonight, I had to get my own taxi anyway. As I did not have a trainee, I didn't go to the crew office and just headed for the taxi rank. There wasn't a queue so I got the first taxi.'

I could see he was not finished. He wanted to make sense of the next part of his reason for getting home that much earlier from a flight, for the first time in nearly thirty years.

'Now you know I don't believe in God. You say you do. Maybe there's someone somewhere taking care of you. Not only did I get the first taxi, I got one that went like stink. He seemed to be in a real hurry. Twice on the expressway I had to ask him to slow down, telling him I wasn't in a hurry. The combination of the early arrival, no trainee, no crew taxi and driver in a hurry made me an hour earlier. That's what happened. That's what saved you,' he said, as hope slowly replaced the weariness in his voice.

'*Saved* me? I did not want to be saved! I am not supposed to be here right now talking to you.' At this point, we both realised that I was not grateful for his early arrival. I did not believe in someone taking care of me. I was no longer sure of the God I prayed to until two nights before. I now wanted to believe that He did not exist.

'I reckon you had two minutes at the most, no more than that. I could not tear that wretched plastic bag. I had to cut it which meant going to the kitchen for the scissors. You were so far gone,' he said. He was very matter-of-fact and calm. I was not sure if the gravity of my actions had sunk in for both of us.

'I chose that bag because it was hard to tear. I was afraid I might panic and try and tear it off.'

'How ironic. It's what kept you alive for that much longer. Because it was not soft, it couldn't mould into all the areas of your face tightly enough to block out all the air. There would have been pockets of air left after the first several minutes which slowed down the whole process. By the time I found you, there was one tiny area of air just at your nostrils. I think that too would have disappeared in a minute,' he explained it as accurately as he saw it.

I sat there, listening, trying to take it all in.

'How could you? How could you not think of the children?' he asked as the anger he kept inside crept into his voice.

I looked away. What had I just put him through? What if I had succeeded? What about the children? The selfishness was incomprehensible to him. I had made two huge mistakes – not allowing time for him to be early and using the wrong type of plastic bag. I was still alive when all I wanted to be was dead.

'I had to wake Ani up to help. I did CPR, and when you were sufficiently alive, Ani and I got you up and dragged you to the lift. On the way to the door, you threw up all over the dining room, by the way,' he said as he attempted to finish the story of how we ended up in hospital.

I wanted him to stop. I did not want to hear another word about being 'saved'.

'I am so sorry, Bob. I am so sorry you had to find me and put up with all this. I swear it was meant to be neat and easy. I should be dead now and I'm so sorry to cause you all this trouble. I am so sorry,' I said, apologising with all my heart. I had no idea what exactly I was apologising for. Putting him through hell? Not dying? I think it was both although dying would have been much worse for him in the beginning.

'Promise me you will never, ever do this again,' he said in a voice exhausted from a long and stressful night.

I was silent. I looked out the window and thought about how suicide had been a recurring thought, seemingly normal, for over thirty years. How can I make a promise I cannot possibly be sure to keep, with all good intentions? I could not tell him this.

'Promise me. Please, you must promise me. If not, how else can I ever fly again?' he asked, his face serious and his voice pleading.

He deserved a promise and he deserved one that was going to

be kept. And I was going to do everything to keep that promise.

'I promise,' I said. I meant it with all the love in my heart for Bob. We were both drained but even then we knew I was going to keep my promise. For him and for the girls, if not for me.

'The minute you become a parent, you revoke the right to think about yourself. You cannot do this to the children. You simply cannot,' he said as he was about to leave. 'They must never know about this.'

By now, it was nearly two-thirty in the morning. He was still in his pilot's uniform minus his epaulettes, tie and the wing badge above his pocket. He got up from my bed, kissed me on my forehead and promised to see me with the girls in the early afternoon.

Soon after he left, I fell asleep.

At about six-thirty in the morning, I woke up. I had left the curtains drawn open and the early dawn light was shining into my room. I called my friend Bina, an early riser with whom I'd had what was supposed to be my last lunch. She had not yet read my email. She started to read it as we spoke.

'Oh my God, Mahits! What happened? Why did you not say anything during lunch? I knew, I just *knew* in my bones something was wrong. Why did I not see it? I'm getting ready and coming over to see you right now,' she said. I liked how she called me Mahits.

I asked her to please get into my email account and to send an email to everyone, explaining that I was going to be fine. I asked her to please apologise on my behalf for the sheer stupidity of my message and actions. I dictated a short note, hung up and tried to go back to sleep.

Instead of trying to sleep, I thought about some of the things I had gotten wrong in the past few years. There were countless mistakes ranging from the inane like burning a pot of rice to more cerebral things like a strategy for a new business pitch. Never had I ever felt like such a failure. Not until now, sitting in my hospital bed dictating a note of apology to people whom I had just bid farewell. I had failed myself and now I had to start all over again. I was going to have lots of support but I needed the will and at that point, I just could not summon it.

At about eight o'clock that morning, a bright and sunny Saturday in November, my friends Bina, Nic and Gerry were at my bedside. By nine o'clock a few other close friends, Catherine and Marida, had arrived. An hour later Monica paid a visit. Another very dear friend, Anne, was in Bangkok for a wedding, but sent a text message to Gerry to say that she would skip the wedding and return that afternoon. Gerry told her I was going to be all right and assured Anne that she should stay for the wedding. I was extremely touched by the care and concern of my friends. At the same time, I was embarrassed for troubling them.

We were all gathered in a room with four beds but I was the only one there. I was in the psychiatric ward of Singapore's newest state hospital. The view was spectacular, overlooking mature green angsana trees, with its plentiful wide deep-green leaves.

My friends, all of whom knew each other, some more than others, kept the conversation light and happy. No one asked me why, no one judged me and at the same time, no one acted as if they needed to be extra gentle. No one walked on eggshells.

Their love and support were both given in abundance and filled the room. I had other friends like that, in Singapore and scattered around the world. In the following years, some friends would matter less or not at all, while others would matter much more.

Gerry bought me a beautifully made notebook bound in purple fabric. She had read that writing was therapeutic for people with bipolar disorder and knew I loved to write. She created a roster where the friends who visited me in hospital would be on duty in case I needed support. I insisted I would be fine but Gerry wanted to be sure and said it was only temporary, maybe two or three weeks until the medication took hold.

I was very happy to see my friends but I was also very tired. They all left at different times, the last saying her goodbyes at eleven that morning. I enjoyed the solitude for a while, had a reasonably good lunch in bed, read a few pages of a book that Catherine had brought as a gift and then slept for an hour.

At about two o'clock, Bob brought the girls. They were a week from turning fourteen and still innocent in so many ways.

'Silly, silly Mummy, drinking champagne with your sleeping pills. Tsk, tsk, tsk. What were you thinking? But you're okay now so we are happy and want you to come home soon,' said the girls cheerily as they showered me with hugs and kisses. I could see beyond the brave front. Later that afternoon, Caroline left for a two-week school trip to Chiang Mai in Northern Thailand. It was essential for her to leave knowing her mother was going to be fine. I promised her I would be.

The nurses came in to check on me every hour. I was heavily sedated. I was terrified of having to go for electroconvulsive therapy, better known as ECT, which I knew I needed. I was wondering if it would start that day itself. The next day, just before I was discharged, a young woman, a doctor with an impeccable bedside manner and a kindly demeanour came and spoke to me.

'You may not feel it, but your body and mind suffered severe trauma and you now need to be gentle with yourself. The next time you get like this, where you're on a precipice, you need to call your doctor immediately. Electroconvulsive therapy would be helpful in a situation like this', she said softly. 'Please take good care of yourself and ensure you take your medication diligently. Every doctor will stress that.'

'Should I start ECT tomorrow, or early next week?'

'I think it is best you discuss treatment options with your doctor,' she said. The hospital must have known I had lied because of the criminal element associated with attempted suicide. They could not prove it and had to accept my explanation. I believed that as a result, I was being sent to my doctor instead of returning for a follow up consultation. I was relieved not to be getting ECT but was afraid I might want to try suicide again. I decided I would see Dr Soh immediately if those bad thoughts of suicide so much as crossed my mind.

The next day, Sunday, I was discharged from hospital and ready to go home. I felt relieved and scared at the same time. I distinctly remember not feeling particularly happy, nor was I sad. I felt nothing. Bob picked me up at the hospital lobby.

When I got home, I had a long shower and went straight to bed. I was numb. I recognised this state of being. It was like being a vegetable, no emotion and no thoughts.

In the first few months following my failed suicide attempt, I often asked myself about divine intervention or a cosmic link to Bob's exceptionally early arrival home that night. The circumstances made sense but the combination of the trainee pilot calling in sick the day before, plus being first in line for the taxi and having a driver who thought he was Superman did not seem random or real. Returning home more than an hour early seemed like a cosmic plan.

I will never know what the universe was doing that night, or what games God was playing, but whenever I doubt the power of the heavens above, my mind rewinds full speed to that night when I wanted to sleep and not wake up ever again.

CHAPTER 10

'Electroconvulsive therapy is not considered for
garden-variety depression. If it's more refractory, if other
treatments have failed or it's suicidal depression, and you
don't have time to wait around to see if a medication is
going to work, it's considered the gold standard of treatment.'
Dr Catherine Birndorf

The hospital put me on medical leave for a week to rest and
recover.

The day after I was discharged, on a wet Monday morning,
I went to the office and headed straight for Sorab's room. I told
him what had happened over the weekend. He looked at me, both
shocked and puzzled, and just listened intently. I remember being
so heavily medicated that I could speak of the whole episode
without emotion.

He told me to take as much time off as I needed. He asked if
my team needed to report to another group account director for
the time being. I said I wanted to continue supporting my account
executives and managers.

I then called a meeting in my room with my team and told them I had to stay at home and rest. I didn't tell them what had happened, just that I was sick.

'I really need you to hold the fort especially on L'Oreal, Tiffany and Lufthansa. Darlie, too, because of the upcoming launch. I'll keep in touch with you while I'm awake during the day. You must, absolutely must, call me if there's a problem you feel you cannot solve. I may not be in the office but you always have my support. You know that.' I assured them that they should not be afraid to call me at home.

As I left the office, I heard a familiar song being played in someone's room. I recognised it at once as 'Drops of Jupiter' by Train. Long before I was diagnosed, I identified with the lyrics when the song was first released a few years earlier and played often on the airwaves. I knew what it felt like to make my way through the constellations and to fall from a shooting star, and yes, the wind did sweep me off my feet and Venus did blow my mind. The song lifted my spirits as I walked out the door towards the lift.

When I returned to the office a week later, I jumped right into my work. December was around the corner which meant a lot of time to be spent on strategic planning and budgeting for all clients. It was going to be busy for the next few months.

Christmas came and went. With the start of the New Year in 2006, I decided that I was going to live my life differently, defining a set of priorities with family always placed first. At work, things ambled along. I no longer drove business development. I was starting to find my equilibrium.

In the middle of February, Bob and I took the girls on a winter holiday to America. While there, I started to experiment with lowering my dosage of Lamotrigine, taking one pill a day instead of two. Dr Soh's words about discipline rang clearly in my head but I decided I could monitor myself closely and try out my new regime for up to a month. It was a very bad idea.

* * *

The condominium in which we lived was up for an en-bloc sale. A hundred and fourteen spacious homes were going to make way for about five hundred smaller apartments. The process of getting residents' approval had started at least six months earlier. Bob never signed the agreement to sell because we did not believe we could find anything better. Also, our children had lived there since they were born and our family had some of the best memories within those walls. We were dead against the sale. The en-bloc committee managed to get the minimum eighty percent approval and the site was opened to tender a few months before. We were very upset but knew we were outnumbered and had to be prepared to move. We expected to hear the result of the tender in April or May. Rumour had it that the sale would go through as the reserve price had been set months earlier when the market was down but prices were now rising quickly.

In early March, Bob and I started looking for a new home. We could not find anything suitable in our price range. We were looking to replace our current apartment, a spacious home with a large balcony or terrace with complete privacy and surrounded by lush greenery. Apartments which fulfilled that set of criteria had either been torn down to make way for new apartments or were in the process of an en-bloc sale with a premium added on to the market rate. The stress of house-hunting was getting to me. There were many homes I liked which were in our price range but Bob always found something wrong. It was either the view or the lack of privacy or the noise from an expressway. He was looking for a perfect place but it did not exist within our budget. I was getting very tired of seeing houses and apartments which I liked but could not buy.

By late March, we received a letter confirming the sale had gone through. The developers were cash-rich so we knew this was for real. I was devastated even though I knew this would happen. I had harboured hopes of the sale falling through. Now I knew for sure we had to leave within a year. This added some urgency to our search.

The Sunday after we received the letter, we saw an apartment at Mount Sinai Rise. It was the second unit in the same block that we had seen. I liked it very much but as soon as I saw Bob's face when he looked towards the greenery in the distance and the high-rise apartment coming up in front, I knew he was not interested. As I stood on the fourteenth floor balcony, I was consumed by an urge to jump. I wanted to die. Just die. I did not feel particularly sad, but I felt hopeless, a feeling which had crept up on me over the past few days since we received the letter. I walked away from the balcony into the living room. Knowing Bob was not interested in the apartment because of the blocked view, I asked to leave immediately as I felt unwell.

In the car, I told Bob what went through my head while I was on the balcony.

'We need to see Dr Soh first thing tomorrow morning.' He was now more aware of the dangers of my reactions and knew exactly how to respond.

The next day, a dreary Monday morning, I made an emergency appointment with Dr Soh. Bob came with me. It was the first time he had accompanied me to the psychiatrist. After what seemed like a brief discussion, Dr Soh decided that I needed electroconvulsive therapy. I was astonished at how quickly he made a decision for such a drastic treatment. In fact, I had visited his office that morning as the perfect candidate for ECT. Such was my determination to die. I had also broken the cardinal rule by not taking my medication diligently.

'Electric shock, just like in the movie *One Flew Over the Cuckoo's Nest*? Did you see that movie? What's so therapeutic about that?' I don't know why I asked those questions or why I asked them with such unnecessary antagonism. Bob patted my thigh in an attempt to calm me down. From the books I had read, I knew exactly what it was and what it entailed. I also knew that for genuinely suicidal patients especially those with a history of attempted suicide, it was the right treatment.

'It is not quite like the electroshock it used to be,' he said trying to reassure me, 'and no, not like in the movie, not at all. That's why we call it electroconvulsive therapy or ECT.' I already knew that. He explained that an anaesthetic and a muscle relaxant would be used before he delivered the electrical stimulus. I smiled when he used the word 'stimulus' for 'shock', positive that the kinder-sounding term came from America. He explained that adverse effects included confusion and short-term memory loss which in most cases returned eventually. *Most* cases. Not all cases; not in every case.

It was a procedure that required me to be hospitalised for a week. Even though I was going to be at a private hospital, which looked more like a hotel with medical services and facilities, I did not want to be left in the mental ward. I was also concerned about the cost which would not be covered by insurance. I begged Dr Soh to allow me to be treated as an outpatient. He relented, but on condition that Bob signed an undertaking that he would always be by my side for the next six days.

'It's about what you said about my responsibility as a mother.

205

I do not get to think about myself anymore. It's why I told you as soon as I felt the urge yesterday. I don't want to destroy our children's lives,' I looked at Bob, grateful he had agreed to stay for my treatment. We both knew it was the only way I could keep my promise to not to try and kill myself again.

Bob agreed to drive me to the hospital on Tuesday morning. As he was scheduled to fly to Sydney that night, he called the crew-scheduling department and asked for emergency time off which was taken from his annual leave. Knowing how sacred annual leave was to him, I apologised profusely for spending it on hospital shuttles and round-the-clock vigil for an undeserving wife. He said it was not a problem; my health was a priority for the whole family.

'Thank you, Bob, that is very kind. It's so typical of you to see things that way,' I said, grateful for his commitment

On each day of the ECT treatment, Bob dropped me off and returned to pick me up. Each time I was disoriented and remembered much less than I did that morning or the night before. By the sixth day, after my third and last ECT session, I had lost all memory of the past week and our recent holiday in America. That was a particularly big blow for me because I had gone to spend a few days with my mother in Los Angeles and had no recollection of my time with her. Nearly six years later, I still have little memory of that holiday. I was sick for several days and felt lifeless for the duration of the treatment. I resented not remembering what we did as a family or what the children said earlier in the week. However, I did not think about wanting to die; not once did it cross my minds for months after ECT.

As it turned out, electroconvulsive therapy was a necessary evil, but in the early days I felt it gave less to me and instead took more out of me. I was alive but I felt cheated. I felt slow and listless. I was not sad but I had stopped laughing. I wanted many things for myself: to get better so I could have my old self back; to be Bob's wife again and the best mother I could possibly be; to cook and bake. I wanted to laugh like I used to.

It was difficult to function in my role at McCann Erickson. Unable to cope with the pace, I resigned. Sorab was, as usual, very kind and accommodating; he tried to convince me to stay and offered to help me get the best possible treatment in New York where the agency was headquartered. I was floored by his largesse, by this person who focused entirely on the strengths and contributions of his employees, while being totally aware of our flaws. Most employers, and I dare say the average Singaporean one, would be celebrating my departure before my seat had time to get cold. I was touched by his very kind and thoughtful offer but had to decline because by then, my senses somewhat dulled, I simply did not recognise the person I had become.

For a few weeks, I stayed at home and did nothing. I did not think about dying or wanting to die. In fact, I just did not think.

CHAPTER 11

'Each human being must keep alight within him the sacred flame
of madness. And must behave like a normal person.'

Paulo Coelho

I do not remember for how long the effects of ECT lasted but I
do remember being very upset about losing my memory of Bob's
birthday celebrations with his mother and the girls. His birthday
lunch was the day after my first session. Even now, six years later,
my memory of that day is a blank despite looking at pictures of
all of us taken that day at the restaurant.

About four weeks after ECT and weeks of expensive
medication – mood stabilisers, anti-psychotics and anti-
depressants – along with psychotherapy, I felt more stable than
I could remember. I did not experience mood swings. What was
noticeable to my family and friends was the absence of strong
emotions. I always looked forward to chicken rice with the family
on Sunday evenings; now it was just a ritual. I enjoyed watching
the girls during their riding lessons; now it was just something
I did as a mother. I loved watching re-runs of *Friends*; now I
switched off the television if I found I could not laugh along with

the canned laughter. At small dinner parties, I was fully engaged in conversations; now I listened with some detachment and could barely contribute a sentence. I neither laughed nor cried.

I was unaware of my new state of being. It was only when my friend, Catherine, always brutally honest with me, mentioned it one day while Bob and I were at a dinner party at her home.

'You've changed. You're not as fun as you used to be,' she said while we were in her kitchen. I was helping her to serve dessert.

'You think so?'

'I'm sure it's your medication. You were more fun when you were bipolar, before medication and certainly before ECT.' I stared at the lemon meringue pie as she sliced it into eight portions. 'Oh, don't look so sad! I'm just saying I miss the old you.' She leaned over the pie, kissed my cheek and proceeded to place each pie on a plate. She then handed me two plates at a time to serve to the guests who were all sitting at the dining table in the balcony.

At around midnight, most of the guests got up to leave. Bob and I stayed for a few more minutes and helped Catherine to clear the table.

'Catherine said I am not as much fun as I used to be,' I said to Bob as soon as we got into the car. 'She thinks it's my medication. Do you think I am boring?'

'I would not say you are boring but you certainly have been very subdued since ECT. It will wear off, you know that. You're on mood stabilisers so you are bound to be a little different from your previous self. You know that, too,' said Bob. 'I would not worry about it if I were you.'

Over the next few days after dinner at Catherine's, I met my friends Anne and Bina separately for lunch and asked if I had become a bore. They both responded similarly – first with surprise at my question and then with honesty about what they experienced. I should not have been surprised to learn that my close friends thought I had become less expressive and my mind was not as quick as it was until the days before ECT. Even when I was in good company, surrounded by family or friends, I appeared a little slow and dull. I was grateful for their candour. I was now aware of the changes in me but I did not know how to undo them. I wondered when, if ever, I would be normal.

The day after my lunch with Anne, I went back to my old research notes and did some new research on medication for bipolar disorder. By now, I had read enough to know that lithium is the most effective long-term treatment for bipolar disorder. As a mood stabiliser, lithium reduces the frequency and severity of mania and also helps relieve depression. It seemed like the perfect medication for me, like an all-in-one pill. I had concerns about the side effects but was willing to try this wonder pill for all the stability it promised.

I was beginning to wonder if there was some truth in what I had heard before about doctors prescribing certain medications based on profit. Not all doctors, just some. I wondered if Dr Soh's hesitation to prescribe lithium despite my repeated requests was due to lithium being cheap and he made a much bigger profit from the other drugs. He eventually agreed to prescribe lithium but he also prescribed expensive multivitamins and other psychotropic drugs. I wanted very much to believe in Dr Soh's good intentions and that the right treatment for me was his priority but over the next few visits I became disenchanted with Dr Soh. I was referred by a friend to another doctor who also diagnosed me as type 1 bipolar and promptly suggested I continue to take lithium.

'Lamotirigine is typically used on type 2 patients. You were not at risk from taking Lamotrigine, don't worry, treatment is just more effective when you're on the right medication. I think lithium is the best treatment for you. Definitely the gold standard for mood stability,' said Dr Ip. 'I will also give you Quetiapine for both the depression and psychosis but take those only when needed.'

With lithium, I was put on yet another medication, and had to brace myself for more side effects. I was given a slow-release lithium pill in four-hundred-milligram dosages and told to start with one a day and then eventually three, the maximum dosage. I did not like the side effects of lithium – dehydration, weight gain, memory loss, trembling hands, nausea and acne – but was encouraged by the doctor to persevere. I had read a lot of good things about lithium and my new-found hero, Dr. Kay Redfield Jamieson – acclaimed author of several non-fiction books on

211

bipolar disorder, including *Exuberance*; Professor of Psychiatry at Johns Hopkins Hospital; international authority on mood disorders – is a staunch advocate, having been on lithium herself for many years.

I persevered and in less than a year I had gained five kilograms and was slightly more than I weighed before my diagnosis. At this point, I was happy for the weight I was putting back on after losing too much when I was first put on medication. A year later I gained another four kilograms, but this was additional weight I neither wanted nor needed. I had gone from a size zero to size six in less than two years. Rather than go on a diet and lose weight, I decided I needed a new outfit every time I could no longer fit into my clothes. Tent dresses became a staple because they were forgiving and allowed room for growth.

With my mood stabilised from lithium, I started to think about getting a job or maybe starting a new business. Within months, I registered an online retail business which subsequently failed. I had a solid business plan and a generous financial backer, my husband, Bob. However, in the process of sourcing things to sell, I learnt that either minimum quantities required per order were too high or lead times were too long. I had a website that was nearly finished but nothing to sell. It was only three months to Christmas. Online retail stores were going to launch their Christmas offerings in a month and I wasn't anywhere close to having anything to sell. I panicked and drastically changed my product mix. Instead of the exquisite handmade artisan things I was going to sell, like ornamental faucets, porcelain wall hooks and hand-painted watering cans, I became just another online retailer selling popular items from mass-market brands. The business was a spectacular failure. Given time, it might have worked but I had dived into what was uncharted territory for me and did not have the patience or the will to see the business through. A very small fraction of Bob's investment was recouped through home sales at drastically reduced prices. The rest of the investment just fizzled into thin air. Bob, the girls, our helper Ani and my small circle of friends were immensely generous and helpful with their time and money. Bob very thoughtfully refrained from making any comments and told me not to worry about the loss. It was a lot of money for us, and I felt like a robber.

Soon after the business folded, my friend Anne, with whom I had worked at Four Seasons, recommended me very highly to her friend, Barbara Maunsell, who was then Vice President Sales and Marketing, Asia Pacific, at Carlson Hotels Worldwide, America's largest privately owned hotel company. I was hired after two interviews.

Carlson, with over two thousand hotels and restaurants, was probably the largest company I ever worked for in terms of volume, but it had a warm, family culture typical of smaller organizations. My colleagues were immensely likeable and senior management was friendly and helpful.

However, even while my mood was stabilised by lithium, I often found it challenging to function in my role as manager of marketing communications for five hotel brands in Asia Pacific. During therapy, barely two months after I started working at Carlson, my doctor suggested that my expectations were probably unrealistic and that I should lower them. She also prescribed a higher dosage of lithium combined with an anti-psychotic every day. This meant having to take the maximum dosage for lithium and start on the minimum dosage for Quetiapine, a drug commonly used to treat acute manic episodes. I took the additional lithium pill but the anti-psychotic made me very sleepy, so I skipped it after a week, which proved to be yet another bad move.

One afternoon, Barbara asked me to do something for The Regent, one of the luxury brands under Carlson at the time. Always mindful of budgets, Barbara suggested options which I felt were more suited to Radisson, a four-star Carlson brand. Unexpectedly I started to yell at her and told her to go find someone else because there was no way I would lower my standards to do anything like what she wanted for a luxury brand. I don't remember what else I said but it must have been peppered with expletives, as my outbursts always are, and I distinctly remember Barbara looking at me with a very kind and calm look on her face while she was in her chair and I stood across her on the other side of her table. I could also sense the deathly stillness in the administrators' island outside her office. By this time, Barbara had already resigned from Carlson and was working through her notice period. When I stopped, she asked me in her softest voice and a rich Australian accent, kind blue eyes looking into mine, 'Want to tell me what's wrong?' She then got up and shut her door.

Trembling with rage, I sat down. I was not afraid about losing my job as I had screamed everywhere I had worked, and with the exceptions of Four Seasons and McCann, no employer ever spoke to me about my behaviour.

I told her I was not well. She looked at me sympathetically and said, 'I know.' I was stunned. What did she mean? What did she know? She looked at me knowingly and I immediately wondered who told her. Instinctively I knew it was not Anne, who would never betray anyone and certainly not me especially after recommending me. I asked Barbara how she knew. She said she really could not tell me but after much probing, I learnt it surfaced during reference checks. By elimination, I knew who it was; I trusted him to have balanced his opinion with positive remarks about my performance.

I could not believe I was having this conversation with Barbara, my boss who had known all along that I was mentally ill and yet hired me. She told me she was familiar with the illness because an acquaintance had it. She also Googled it after interviewing me to learn more about bipolar disorder. In my mind I was thinking she was either very brave or slightly insane herself to hire me.

'I am so sorry for that tantrum, Barbara. But why? Why

would you want to hire someone who starts off as a potential liability?' I asked, baffled and grateful at the same time. My rage had dissipated as quickly as it had risen. Barbara's kind and gentle manner had a soothing effect on me.

'Anne said you were the right person and I could stop looking. I have known Anne for a very long time and I trust her judgement.' She said it so matter-of-factly as if to ask why I was surprised. I felt I was in the presence of a giant.

She had chosen to focus on my strengths and totally ignored my one serious and potentially dangerous flaw, planning to cross the bridge when she reached it. And cross the bridge she did in just six months, with exceptional grace.

Barbara returned to her home in Sydney a week later. She was replaced by a man from another departmentnamed Kurt. Since joining Carlson, I found Kurt to be smart and focused. I looked forward to working with him but it soon became evident that we were not going to have a good working relationship. This was triggered by the regular arguments I had over the phone when dealing with colleagues from various cities in Asia. It boiled down to my unrealistic expectaions when trying to impose production standards, specifically what makes a good photograph or advertisement or brochure. I reminded myself constantly 'This is not Four Seasons, not Ogilvy, not Tiffany & Co.' After being spoilt working with the number ones, I believed that the problem was mine – I expected far too much.

After Barbara left, I managed to last another eighteen months mainly because I chose to align myself with a handful of bright, competent peers from other departments, all of whom had a great sense of humour. One afternoon while trying for the umpteenth time to get better quality images for the corporate directory, I had a massive outburst over the phone with one of my overseas colleagues. Kurt called me in and reprimanded me. Although officially I resigned that day, for all intents and purposes I was fired. It really was about time for me to leave anyway. To survive Carlson I had to supplement my maximum lithium dosage with an anti-psychotic at least once – ideally twice – a day but I could not deal with the initial side effects of anti-psychotics. Losing my job at Carlson was the price I paid for my refusal to take anti-psychotics.

After I left Carlson, I considered my options and thought about starting another business. It was tempting but I just could not bear the thought of squandering Bob's hard-earned money the year before the girls started university in England.

By now, I was back down to two lithium pills a day, a third off the dosage from the maximum. Bob did not put any pressure on me to get another job. Our twin daughters were about to begin their long summer holidays, after which they were going to begin their final year of high school. It was going to be a tough and stressful year preparing for their International Baccalaureate exams. I wanted to dedicate myself to the welfare and comfort of our daughters in their last year of high school. I decided I would drive them to and from activities like riding, chemistry tuition and music lessons. It would save them precious time taking the train or the bus or even waiting for taxis, time that could be spent relaxing at home or catching up on homework or studying. I would take them out for ice cream just for fun. I would be there when they came home on the school bus and listen when they spoke about their day. I was going to be a full-time mother, focusing entirely on the girls. Before long it became clear that while I was doing all this ostensibly for the children, I was actually doing it for myself, making up for lost time and giving myself much happiness in the process.

The motherhood make-up time lasted a year and I loved it. I was happy. More than that, I was contented. I did not experience extreme mood swings. During this phase of normalcy, I wondered about what I would do once the girls left for university and Bob started flying more often in a bid to see them in England.

I thought I would spend some time on the spiritual island of Bali and let the heavenly powers on the island decide my future for me. I visited Bali for the first time in 1999, during a summer holiday with the family. We spent nearly two weeks in various areas. There was something special about Bali on that first visit; I knew I wanted to return again and again. For the next ten years we visited Bali every year, sometimes just for five days. By my third visit, I felt a strong desire to live in Bali someday but never gave it much thought upon returning home after each visit. Bob and the girls noticed that I was much calmer when I was in Bali, more so than anywhere in the world we went on holiday. Just as England brought out the worst in me because of the weather and what I sometimes found to be disagreeable food, Bali brought out the best in me because of the weather and the excellent restaurants. More than that, it was the Balinese with their warmth and friendliness that drew me to their paradise. In late 2009, about a month before we left for a holiday in Bali, I lined up a few villas to view. I spoke to Bob about my plans one afternoon.

'I'd like to go house-hunting while we're in Bali. I'll be forty-seven in two weeks. I don't see myself getting a suitable job here at this age. I'll go stir-crazy while the girls are away and you're busy with work. I can't do the *tai-tai* thing, it's so not me,' It dawned on me during this conversation that I had considered spending most of my time in Bali without even giving Bob a hint of my plans. This was the first time he was hearing about it.

'Why Bali? What would you do there? We can't afford to run two households,' Bob said, alarmed that I would be so decisive about such a drastic change in our lives. 'Have you been skipping your medication?' He was concerned that I was entering a manic phase, seeing my plan as a delusion of grandeur which was very likely to end in failure.

'I was thinking I would buy a villa and run a hosted bed and breakfast like the ones in Europe and Australia where the owner lives on-property. It will be luxurious. I checked on the Internet and could not find anything like it in Bali. This might well be Bali's first luxury hosted bed and breakfast. You know I love Bali, you know I'd love to live there. Why not now?' I asked, unable to see any problem with my plan. 'I have been very good about my medication, by the way. This is not mania talking, it is me preparing for life as an empty nester.'

'I'm very concerned that you are jumping into something you know very little about. It could cost us a lot of money and with the girls about to go to university and my retirement not too far away, we can't take such risks,' said Bob.

'You're right. It is a huge risk. I'm just looking at what's available and at what price. It's not like I will see something and make an offer. Besides, I would not do anything without first talking to you,' I said. 'Don't worry, I will do a lot of research before we leave. Promise.'

In the eight days that we were there, I ended up viewing nearly twenty villas, mostly overpriced because Julia Roberts had just landed to film *Eat, Pray, Love*. What was available within our budget was mostly built to the hilt on small plots of land and closed in with high walls. It was not how I wanted to live on a tropical island. By the time I had seen twelve villas, the real estate agent, a young American named Eric, asked if I wanted to consider increasing my budget. I spoke to Bob about it that evening. We went through the websites of the three top real estate agencies in Bali and realised we had to double the amount to get a decent-sized villa, which meant at least fifteen thousand square feet of land, in a good location, which meant the villa enclaves in the south western part of Bali.

With this new budget, I was able to view eight excellent villas over the next two days. The last one Eric showed me had spectacular views of lush terraced rice fields and sat on a plot of nearly half an acre of land. This was it. I felt it in my bones just as I had with Bob nearly thirty years earlier. The villa was a lot more than we were first prepared to pay and much bigger than was needed for a bed and breakfast but there was something about it that made me desire this particular villa.

When I got back to the hotel, I told Bob about it. It was just within our new budget but we needed to set aside another twenty percent on top of the purchase price for legal fees and renovations.

'You were supposed to be looking, just checking out the options. You weren't going to buy right away! Please don't get carried away with this.' His voice was tinged with annoyance. This was all too quick and unexpected for both of us. I shared Bob's concern about finances but felt so strongly about the villa and it's suitability for a luxury bed and breakfast.

'It's perfect for a luxury bed and breakfast. I've checked various websites and can't find a luxury bed and breakfast where the owner or manager lives at the villa. Lots of guest houses and some hosted bed and breakfasts but they are certainly not luxurious. It's a good thing to do. Please, Bob?' I begged him to trust me on this venture.

A month later, just before Christmas, we paid the twenty percent deposit and were on our way to owning a villa in Canggu, one of Bali's premier residential districts. The girls were thrilled about having a second home in Bali.

The next step was to take ownership in April 2010. The previous owner was already committed to a long-term rental and could not release the villa any earlier. Soon after ringing in the new year, I began the task of looking for renovation contractors and decorators. A former colleague from Singapore who had built a house in Bali was extremely helpful with recommendations, including landscapers and pest control companies.

While I was in Bali discussing the scope of work with the contractor, I learnt that they were going to be more extensive than I had envisaged and would cost more. Bob and my friends were concerned about how I would cope with the renovations. We had all renovated our homes and knew what it entailed, even with what we believed were the best contractors. Renovating a home is extremely stressful and time-consuming. Murphy's Law prevails in every situation – what can go wrong, will go wrong. My doctor insisted I get back on the maximum dosage of lithium supplemented by anti-psychotics. Everyone I knew was worried about how I would cope with the stress.

I had the misfortune of working with a contractor who was

actually very competent but had taken on far too many projects and could not cope with his limited resources. He had certainly talked the talk. I was taken in by the fact that he was Western, articulate and I believed he would understand my needs and preferences better. Also, he seemed like a gentleman. Things progressed quite well in the beginning but he was taking on more and more work at other villas and areas he had agreed to repair were now left untouched. Also, some jobs were badly done and problems surfaced barely three months later. His men were never available to fix them. I eventually had to call in other contractors. This meant more time and a lot more money. I was already back on the maximum dosage of lithium a month after moving to Bali. I had taken Quetiapine a few times in the previous two weeks, the tiny pink pill containing the badly needed anti-psychotic that had protected those around me in my manic moments. Each time it transported me into the deepest chemically induced sleep only to be rudely awakened by workmen banging on my door and asking what to do when clear instructions had already been given a few times.

So much for peace and tranquillity. The Indonesians are a very gentle and polite people; the spiritual Balinese even more so. They do have their moments of aggressiveness and some can even be violent but when faced with a hysterical woman, they are dumbfounded. They seriously believed I was possessed when I screamed one day about the hideous green on the garden walls. I had chosen the colour but they were supposed to test the colour on a small area first. I asked them why they skipped that step. They just shrugged their shoulders. Needless to say, I had to pay for both the paint and the workmanship to repaint the entire wall, all six thousand square feet of it. The manic rages were getting too frequent so I forced myself to take Quetiapine daily, sleeping for an hour and making it through the day subdued and feeling heavily drugged but at least I was not suicidal.

Five months after signing the deeds, the villa was fully renovated and refurbished. Photography was completed in three days and the website was launched soon after. Villa Juno, named for my beloved mother-in-law, welcomed its first guests in late September 2010.

As much as I loved Bali, and had often considered it for retirement, I could not have foreseen myself moving there quite so soon. For all its spirituality and tranquillity, for all its spellbinding magic, I had flown into a manic rage at least six times in as many months and each time it was with different people in a different situation but the response was always the same – a bewildered look on their kind faces followed by a desire to leave in a hurry.

The villa was full over Christmas week. The early months of the next year were slow, and then business picked up again in May. Bob and the girls visited a few times, spending between three days and a week each time.

It was tiring at times but rewarding especially when guests

left at the end of their vacation offering most sincere gratitude for a memorable stay. Some guests posted reviews on Tripadvisor without being asked to; at one point, in April 2011, Villa Juno catapulted to number one out of seventeen bed and breakfasts in Canggu on Tripadvisor and top fifteen out of nearly four hundred bed and breakfasts in Bali.

My lithium dosage remained the same, at four hundred milligrams, twice a day. I had a team of competent and wonderful staff with whose support I was better equipped to manage some of our more demanding guests and the day-to-day challenges that arose from shoddy maintenance or workmanship typical in Bali, exacerbated by living in the middle of rice fields – from back-up generators that fail during a power-cut to baby monitor lizards lounging not far from the swimming pool and garden snakes slithering toward a pool chair while a guest sunbathed.

The environment and slower pace of life made me feel calmer although I still had my manic moments. For days on end I was happy and contented yet there were times when my staff wondered if I had been possessed by spirits.

I came to accept the fact that regardless of my lithium dosage and where I lived, I would float between periods of normalcy and manic depression. However, the scales seemed tipped in my favour in Bali for it was there I felt my best more often and with greater intensity.

I wanted to spend the rest of my life at Villa Juno.

CHAPTER 12

'I am the master of my fate: I am the captain of my soul.'
William Ernest Henley, *Invictus*

Nearly two years after I moved to Bali, I found out from my staff that the rice field immediately to the left of Villa Juno had been sold and that construction of a cluster of villas would begin around July 2012. I also learnt from a neighbour that three large villas were to be built on the field to the right of Villa Juno. With rampant construction about to begin to the left, right and directly in front, just beyond the walls of Villa Juno, I knew that my rustic tranquillity was about to disappear. I was hesitant to take bookings from July onwards; I was afraid of the demands for refunds due to construction noise. I was most afraid of bad reviews on Tripadvisor. I knew I had to put the villa up for sale immediately.

That weekend, several agents visited the villa. I signed agreements for listings on their respective websites. Every agent warned me that the market was very competitive. There were nearly a hundred villas for sale in the Canggu area alone and limited cash-rich buyers, the majority of whom were Indonesians looking for distressed sales. I was mentally prepared for a slow sale at a loss, so nothing could have prepared me for the break-neck speed at which I went from an offer to leaving my sanctuary. I did not have time to contemplate life after Villa Juno.

The villa was sold within weeks of going on the market. The whole process was fast-tracked by the buyer's lawyer for completion in ten days. This was possible because the buyer was Indonesian and my papers were in perfect order.

I asked for at least a month for completion so I could send last-minute invitations to my friends to visit Villa Juno before I moved to another villa in Bali. I also needed time to find a new place. The buyer and I agreed on completing the sale in early March on the condition that I was allowed to stay rent-free until the end of March. Within days of the sale agreement being signed, the owner began to make unreasonable demands about the payment terms. I pointed out that buyers do not get to dictate payment terms and he had already agreed to my terms which were in keeping with industry standards. During the extremely unpleasant exchanges which bordered on harassment in the few days before the actual day of completion of the sale, my mind was in turmoil. I was physically ill. I decided I could not stay at Villa Juno as a favour from a person whom I believed tormented me for days. While the buyer assumed I would stay until the end of the month, which was three weeks away, I gave myself no more than five days; barely time to get my tax returns completed and most of my belongings packed.

It was late Friday afternoon by the time the transfer deeds were signed and the money paid. I returned to Villa Juno from the notary's office and did an inventory check with the buyer and his family. Over the weekend, I packed whatever was not part of the inventory and had them sent to my driver's home for storage. I filled up all my tax forms and sent them to the tax consultant on Monday morning. By three o'clock on Tuesday afternoon, I had signed all my tax returns in Denpasar and made all the necessary payments. I headed back to the villa. Heart heavy and mind spinning, I called Bob from the car and asked him to arrange a ticket on the next flight back to Singapore.

At five o'clock on a Tuesday afternoon, I left for the airport and boarded the last Singapore Airlines flight that day. It had been barely two weeks since I accepted the offer and four days since I sold the villa.

* * *

It took weeks to recover from the shock of leaving my sanctuary without allowing myself to be mentally and physically prepared, without the joy of making the most of my last few days in Bali. I maintained my lithium dosage and supplemented it with Quetiapine which treats both psychosis and depression. I spent most of my time at home. A few days after my arrival from Bali, Caroline returned from England for Easter break. I was happy in her company and knew I would soon be all right. I slowly started to see a few friends and weaned myself off Quetiapine after three weeks.

* * *

In early April, I went to Guangzhou for Qing Ming. If Amah were still alive, she would be a hundred years old. Xun, Amah's grandson, borrowed his friend's car and drove me around all weekend. He introduced me to his wife, while his sister introduced me to her husband and son. Our first stop was the columbarium in Panyu, Amah's village. We lit joss sticks and burnt paper offerings for Amah, her late husband and her late son, Xun's father. After the ritual, I wiped clean Amah's urn and her designated cubicle before placing the urn back inside.

Mrs Huang, Amah's widowed daughter-in-law, held court during all our lunches and dinners as a family that weekend. Over a ten-course dinner prepared by Mrs Huang's son-in-law at Xun's home, Mrs Huang spoke of Amah's dementia in her last years; Amah believed I was visiting her and would regularly ask her son, my elder brother Go Go, to take her to the port in Panyu so she could welcome me. It broke my heart to imagine Amah waiting for me only to go home disappointed.

That evening, I learnt that Amah was not a Guan Yin worshipper nor would she have believed in cures by a temple medium. Her family and I agreed Amah may have been given the statue I remembered from my childhood and kept it as an ornament. As for the temple medium she spoke about, Amah may have heard about that option from her friends. We can never be sure about Amah's beliefs but all that mattered then were my fond memories of her. It was a privilege for me to be with her family whose own memories of Amah enriched mine.

Feeling uplifted while with Amah's family, I stopped taking Quetiapine on my first night in Guangzhou. Three days later, when I left Guangzhou, both Elena and Caroline met me at Changi Airport. I was not expecting to see Elena until a day or two later. She told me she had taken an earlier flight just so she could be at the airport to meet me on my return from Guangzhou. I was overjoyed. For a moment, while walking to the taxi stand with Caroline and Elena, telling them about Amah's family and the memories we shared, I thought I felt the euphoria of mania wrap around me like a soft silk shawl. I did not reach for Quetiapine. Instead I enjoyed every blissful minute of my first two days back in Singapore with the girls.

* * *

About a month after I returned from Guangzhou, I thought about getting another villa in Bali. I wanted to re-create the Villa Juno experience in another part of the island. I spoke to several agents about what was available. Hosted bed and breakfasts, many claiming to be luxurious, had sprung up all over the popular tourist areas. Eventually I decided I would hold off returning to Bali for a while. After spending so much time with Bob and our daughters, I realised how much I had missed my family. I wanted to be in Singapore when the girls returned for their ten-week summer break.

My mind could not plan anything beyond then.

CHAPTER 13

'I am interested in madness. I believe it is the biggest
thing in the human race, and the most constant.
How do you take away from a man his madness
without also taking away his identity?'
William Saroyan

I spent a significant part of my life feeling different, *being* different,
only to be told it had all to do with a chemical imbalance in my
brain. It was a life-changing revelation to learn there was an
explanation and a name for my unusual behaviour.

I walked out of the doctor's office after my second diagnosis
with bags of pills and a heart full of hope for a quieter mind only to
learn that the psychosis and melancholia do come back. However,
since starting on lithium, I have spent the last five years living
with longer and more frequent periods of normalcy. The manic
episodes are few and far between, while the suicidal thoughts are
extremely rare. When I feel I am about to be consumed by a high
or low wave, I know I must take a supplementary pill and I do,
usually Quetiapine, sometimes Alprazolam (commonly sold as

Xanax). I carry these little pills with me in my wallet.

I have learnt to manage this dreaded illness which has, according to some studies, a completed suicide rate of up to twenty percent and an attempted suicide rate of up to fifty percent. I am now a statistic in the latter and do not wish to be part of the former.

* * *

I lived for the most part like anyone I knew. I have always kept a very small circle of precious friends, some new and some old; I had a job, even though I did hop around a little but no more than many people I know; I got married and I raised two children while juggling a career. I sat on the Committee of the Society for the Prevention of Cruelty to Animals for twelve years and only stepped down when I moved to Bali. As a voracious reader, I co-founded a book club with two friends and have been running it for eight years. SPCA and book club evenings were a priority for me; I always felt nourished by the few people who were there. I loved having dinner parties at home. I liked going to the movie theatre; loved to eat, especially Singapore street food; enjoyed watching television and even had my favourite comedy and drama series. Like most women I know, I made an effort to look nice and enjoyed going to salons for my hair, face, hands and feet. I was often happy and sometimes I was sad. At times I felt very confident and at times I was insecure. I was just like everyone else I knew.

Unlike everyone else, however, I was also either manic or suicidal. My emotions were extreme. My exuberance, my anguish, my zeal, my lethargy, my passion and my fury were equally exaggerated. Before I was diagnosed, I sometimes wondered if my extreme moods were due to nothing but a great and innate desire for histrionics. If only. To blame it on chemical imbalance makes it sound so scientific, so logical and therefore easier to forgive all the hurtful words delivered with an even more hurtful tone. Whatever went on in my head before I was diagnosed and put on medication was, at best, fetid and at worst, destructive. The realisation that chemicals in my brain can be so out of whack that it makes me toxic as a person, even for a moment, makes me feel deeply flawed.

Then again, I ask myself, am I really flawed? It has been a gift to experience the level of confidence I have had, never having to consider the source. The boundless energy and bursts of creativity and intelligence which some people interpreted as unbridled passion or an irritating exuberance saw me through many years in the best agencies in the advertising industry, working on the world's leading brands, and made me valued by my employers and clients that mattered. So valued that I had work schedules rearranged to suit my needs at a top advertising agency. My friends, none with mental disorders, are immensely likeable and best described as truly amazing; some friendships go as far back as my teens. This year, Sue and I will both turn fifty and celebrate forty years of friendship.

Bipolar disorder is probably the most romanticised illness because of its association with famous and highly regarded people, from presidents and musicians to actors and writers. The tragic deaths of Van Gogh, Virginia Woolf and Kurt Cobain; the poignant confessions from Churchill and Lincoln which told of stretches of unbearably dark days; the very public meltdown experienced by Bobby Brown and Stephen Fry; the brilliance of Beethoven, Tolstoy and Mark Twain; the trail of chaos and destruction that once followed Russell Brand. The stunning actress, Catherine Zeta-Jones was recently added to a list that goes on. The media feed their audience with such stories, leaving them hungry for more. It is very challenging to convey the devastation that mental illness inflicts upon sufferers and those who are close to them when the media play up the association of mental illness with celebrities. Also, movies like *Blue Sky* and *Mr Jones* portray romance and sentimentality while downplaying, perhaps unintentionally, the harsh realities and the harrowing effects of bipolar disorder. In 2012, the illness was somewhat glamorized when Claire Danes won a Golden Globe for Best Actress in a Television Series (Drama) for her accurate and intelligent portrayal of Carrie Mathison, a passionate and adventurous Central Intelligence Agency agent with bipolar disorder.

There is nothing romantic or glamorous about any kind of

mental illness. Yet I sometimes wonder if people might be attracted to madness at some level. Could they be seduced by something they see, perhaps a quality they do not have but wish they did? Maybe the teacher who saw the devil in my eyes saw a fire that she never knew was possible in a human being. Or maybe it is just that little unexplainable something that Mother Nature gave me in return for getting the formula wrong in my brain.

I am no raving beauty but I got myself a most eligible bachelor when I was just twenty. Bob is very reserved and conservative but he was attracted to me, to what he called my sparkling personality. He stood by me through the days of frightening rages, weeks of melancholia and electroconvulsive therapy. In the early years, he was quick to put those episodes behind him and indulge in the pleasure of my manic highs. Although I never promised him a rose garden, I never thought I could create such havoc. I plan to keep those mercurial days behind us. For good.

Without qualifications to speak of, I was hired for almost every job after being called for an interview. Neil Jacobs, who gave me the five-minute interview for the coveted position at Four Seasons Hotels and Resorts, who had me thinking I had blown it, said to me years later that he just *knew*. He didn't know what it was at first and thought it was instinct. He then mentioned my confidence and my candour. He also mentioned spirit. I could not understand how that was possible in five minutes. He said that in less than two minutes, he knew I was the right person for the job and for Four Seasons, conservative though it was and still is.

Advertising is the perfect industry to camouflage a mental illness like bipolar disorder. Even in its most severe form, type 1, it is possible to hide it. I learnt a long time ago that ultimately it doesn't matter who you are; at work, it is the performance that matters above all else. I had the energy, the drive and the smarts to be very good at what I did. More than that, I was completely engaged at work, always aiming to give one hundred percent. Maybe that's why I crashed every now and then.

If asked to describe me in one word, many former employers and colleagues would probably say hardworking or passionate. Detractors would probably say crazy.

Sparkling personality. Confidence. Candour. Spirit. Light. Passion. Crazy. Something. Whatever. It was mania pure and simple. Some people loved it. They were drawn to it without knowing why.

There are many things I have done of which I am not proud, and many more of which I am very proud, raising good children being my most important achievement. If I could turn back the clock there are several things I would change if I could, and how I wish I could. For all the good and the bad experiences, I am not entirely sure I would change my madness.

After all, as famously asked by the writer William Saroyan, 'How do you take away from a man his madness without also taking away his identity?'

Acknowledgements

Countless people have enhanced my life. I am thankful to all of them. A few others deserve special mention for gifts that go far beyond the usual definitions of friendship and professionalism, never expecting anything in return:

Anne Arrowsmith and Sangeeta Mulchand. Thank you for reading various versions of my manuscript. Your honesty, support and advice helped to make this book happen.

In alphabetical order, friends whose kindness and unwavering loyalty have helped me through my toughest times: Alison David, Asha Hague, Bina Maniar, Deirdre Moss, Geraldine Loh, Goh Poh Sun, Graham Kelly, Juliana Chia, Liz Chew, Mabel Lennhag, Marida Andersen, Meena Jadwani, Monica Alsagoff, Neeta Lachmandas, Nicola Yeo, Patricia Teo, Parizad Setna, Poonam Purshotamdas, Saira & Sunder Kimatrai, Sng Chor Ee, Vivek Dadlani and Ylita Garland.

In chronological order, colleagues and clients – some of whom have since become dear friends – who were not only kind to me but also gave me every opportunity to be the best that I could be and without whose support I would surely have foundered along the way: Lambert Yeo, Emily Koh, Linda Sim, Valarie Chu, Trina Lim, Dave Camacho (RIP), Shamala Ratnam, Michael Chong, Chris Ang, Celestine Yeo, Donna Chua, Nalini Naidu, Philip Hartas, Robert Tan, John O'Shea, Valarie Lim, Kwan Weng Hung, Kathy O'Brien, Jonathan Sicroff, Neil Jacobs, Cherry Kam, Claudia Lam, Paul Iacovino, Ana Sardinha, Sorab Mistry, Susie Lim, Neeraj Mehra, Nicci Gallo, Priyanti Budiono, Elisabeth Teo, Yong Han Ming, Hew Yee Min, Ailynn Seah, Barbara Maunsell, Xerxes Meher-Homji, Julian Meyer and Jan Jansen.

In chronological order, teachers and fellow students from Katong Convent whose kindness and generosity made it easier to get through the difficult years in secondary school: Mrs Rosie Lee, Ms Aileen Lau (RIP), Beatrice Tan, Lucy Tan, Wee Geok Eng, Feni Hartolo, Eleanor Bangar and Wee Hong Beng.

My lovely young friend Alessandra David for the cover art on this book.

A most amazing Book Club of interesting and wonderful people who expanded my literary tastes and with whom I have enjoyed a warm friendship – Anne, Christy, Leesa, Neeta, Nicci, and Vinita.

My sister for encouraging me to get myself checked for bipolar disorder, my mother for her understanding and my aunt, Pushpa, for being all that she has been to me.

Amah's family in China, specifically Go Go and his family. Thank you for accepting me as a member of your family and for helping me to keep Amah's memory alive.

My publisher Philip Tatham at Monsoon Books for believing in my book.

Last but not least, over and above everyone else, I am deeply grateful to the most important people in my life – my husband and our twin daughters. I can never thank them enough.